THE ULTIMATE Disney PARTY BOOK

THE ULTIMATE Disney PARTY BOOK

WRITTEN BY JESSICA WARD
WITH CYNTHIA LITTLEFIELD

PHOTOGRAPHY BY CLARE BARBOZA
FOOD STYLING BY JULIE HOPPER

EDDA USA

The Ultimate Disney Partybook
© 2015 by Disney Enterprises Inc. and Pixar Animation Studios

The Ultimate Disney Party Book is produced by becker&mayer!, Bellevue, Washington.
www.beckermayer.com

Authors: Jessica Ward, Cynthia Littlefield
Design: Sara Baynes
Editors: Dana Youlin, Tinna Proppe, tinna@eddausa.com
Photographer: Clare Barboza
Food Stylist: Julie Hopper
Layout: Olafur Gudlaugsson
Printing: Printed in Slovenia

Distributed by Midpoint Book Sales & Distribution

ISBN: 978-1-94078-704-6

www.eddausa.com

CONTENTS

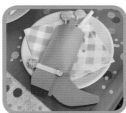

INTRODUCTION

There is nothing more exciting for a kid than an upcoming birthday party—the cake, the friends, the games, the presents! But for a parent, planning a successful party presents a challenge. Keeping things fun, delicious, and easy can be tricky. Fortunately, you don't need a magic lamp or the help of a Fairy Godmother to plan and execute a fantastic birthday party. All you'll need are the ideas contained in this book—along with some craft supplies and a grocery list—and you'll be poised to throw a Disney birthday party that will instantly transform you into your child's hero (and have all the other parents asking for your advice!).

Whether you have a five-year-old daughter who loves *Cinderella* and *The Little Mermaid* or an eight-year-old son who loves *Toy Story* and *Monsters,* *Inc.,* you will find the perfect fully conceived party plan within these pages. Each chapter contains instructions for invitations, decorations, crafts, activities, and recipes—all celebrating favorite Disney and Disney·Pixar characters and films. Flying Carpet Invitations, a Hidden Mickey Scavenger Hunt, Mike Wazowski Cupcakes, the "I'm Gonna Wreck It!" Penthouse Piñata, and Belle's French Baguette Sandwiches are just a sampling of the projects that are presented with detailed, yet easy-to-follow instructions, inspirational artwork, and photographs of the finished product.

After the inevitable success of your child's Disney birthday party, you will have magical memories to share for years to come—and, hopefully, some leftover Mickey sandwich cookies, too!

ALADDIN
PARTY

Aladdin was released in 1992 during the second golden age of Disney animation and is now considered a classic. A reinterpretation of a tale from *One Thousand and One Nights*, the film tells the story of a poor "street rat" who yearns for a better life. In a chance encounter, Aladdin meets the spirited Princess Jasmine in the Agrabah marketplace and resolves to win her heart. With the help of the Genie, Abu, and a flying carpet, Aladdin defeats the evil vizier Jafar, proves himself to be a "diamond in the rough," and earns the love of the princess.

This party plan captures the magic and whimsy of the film, starting with Flying Carpet Invitations, complete with golden tassels. The fun continues with a costume craft: Jasmine's Jeweled Headbands and Aladdin Fezzes. Once the guests are decked out Agrabah-style, it's time for a game of Musical Magic Carpets, set to the *Aladdin* soundtrack, of course! Little princes and princesses can then quench their thirst with Blue Genie Punch, nosh on Animals of Agrabah Pita Chips and Hummus, and go ape for Abu's Caramel Apples. And no party would be complete without a favor—in this case, Diamond in the Rough Rock Candy with Magic Lamp nametags.

FLYING CARPET INVITATIONS

MATERIALS

- 2 (12 IN BY 12 IN) SHEETS PURPLE CARD STOCK
- 2 (12 IN BY 12 IN) SHEETS BRIGHT YELLOW CARD STOCK
- 2 (12 IN BY 12 IN) SHEETS MEDIUM BLUE CARD STOCK
- 24 (8 MM BY 13 MM) TEARDROP-SHAPED YELLOW STICK-ON RHINESTONES
- 12 (8 MM BY 13 MM) TEARDROP-SHAPED SILVER STICK-ON RHINESTONES
- 24 (6 MM) ROUND RED STICK-ON RHINESTONES
- YELLOW YARN OR EMBROIDERY FLOSS
- 6 ENVELOPES (OPTIONAL)

TOOLS:

- PENCIL
- RULER
- SCISSORS
- ULTRA FINE POINT BLACK PERMANENT MARKER
- GLUE TAPE (DOUBLE-SIDED ADHESIVE) APPLICATOR WITH NARROW TIP OR GLUE STICK
- HOT GLUE GUN
- PAPER CUTTER (OPTIONAL)

NOTE → The materials can be scaled up for the number of guests invited to your party.

Upon entering the Cave of Wonders, Aladdin discovers a flying carpet, which becomes one of his faithful companions. It's the ideal mode of transportation—and the perfect emissary for this birthday party. Complete with tassels, these little carpets are made with card stock, stick-on rhinestones, and a touch of magic.

INSTRUCTIONS

STEP 1   Using a pencil, ruler, and scissors—or a paper cutter if preferred—cut out a 7-by-4½ inch rectangle from the purple card stock.

STEP 2   Cut out a 6-by-3½-inch rectangle from the yellow card stock.

STEP 3   Cut out a 5¾-by-3¼-inch rectangle from the blue card stock. Reserve any spare paper.

STEP 4 Use the ultra fine point marker to write all necessary information in the center of the blue rectangle. This should include location, date, time, and RSVP instructions.

STEP 5 Using the glue tape or glue stick, apply adhesive around the edges of the blue rectangle. Place it, centered, on top of the yellow rectangle. There should be a ⅛-inch border of yellow showing on all sides of the blue.

STEP 6 Using the glue tape or glue stick, apply adhesive to the back of the yellow rectangle and center on top of the purple rectangle. There should be a ½-inch border of purple showing on all sides of the yellow.

STEP 7 For each invitation, you will need six teardrop stick-on rhinestones—four yellow and two silver—as well as four round red rhinestones. Place one yellow teardrop in each corner of the blue rectangle, with the narrow end of the rhinestone pointing inward. Place one silver teardrop at the center of each narrow end of the card, narrow end pointing inward. Place one round red rhinestone on each side of the silver teardrops.

STEP 8 To make the tassels, cut a piece of spare card stock measuring 1 inch wide by 2 to 3 inches long. Wrap the yellow yarn around the 1-inch side four times. Cut the yarn tail. Cut another piece of yarn about 2 inches long. Thread it underneath the loops on the card stock strip and then tie it around the wraps to secure them. Slide the loops off the card stock. Cut another piece of yarn about 2 inches long. Wrap the yarn four times around the loops (including the yarn that was used to secure them) about a third of the way from the top of the loops. Tie a knot and pull tight. Snip off the

excess close to the knot. Snip the bottoms of the loops so the strands of the tassel will hang loose. Create four tassels for each invitation.

STEP 9 With a hot glue gun, apply a small amount of glue to the back (knotted side) of the tassel and adhere to the corner of the magic carpet. Cool completely before placing in envelopes, if using.

JASMINE'S JEWELED HEADBAND AND ALADDIN'S FEZ

MAKES 1 HEADBAND AND 1 HAT

MATERIALS

JASMINE'S JEWELED HEADBAND:

- 1 (1 IN LONG) OVAL BLUE FAUX GEMSTONE OR RHINESTONE
- 1 (1½ IN SQUARE) SHEET BLUE CARD STOCK
- GOLD METALLIC DIMENSIONAL FABRIC PAINT
- 1 (36 IN) LENGTH BLUE SATIN RIBBON, ⅝ IN WIDTH

ALADDIN'S FEZ:

- 1 (8 OZ) CIRCULAR PLASTIC STORAGE CONTAINER
- 1 (13 IN BY 4 IN) RECTANGLE OF RED FELT
- 1 (3 IN) CIRCLE OF RED FELT
- 1 (12 IN) LENGTH METALLIC GOLD WAVY TRIM
- 1 (22 IN) LENGTH METALLIC GOLD ELASTIC CORD

TOOLS:

- PENCIL
- RULER
- SCISSORS
- HOT GLUE GUN

NOTE → The materials can be scaled up for the number of guests invited to your party.

Transform your party guests with Agrabah-inspired headwear: Jasmine's jeweled headband and Aladdin's red fez. Each headpiece requires only a handful of materials and will transport partyguests to a whole new world!

INSTRUCTIONS

JASMINE'S JEWELED HEADBAND

STEP 1 Place a blue jewel on top of the blue card stock. Use a pencil to trace around the gem, adding about 2 millimeters to the circumference all around the gem. Cut out the oval.

STEP 2 Apply a small amount of hot glue to the back of the gem and adhere it to the center of the card stock oval. Squeeze a generous bead of metallic gold dimensional fabric paint onto the lip of card stock, surrounding the gem entirely. Let dry for four hours.

STEP 3 Apply a small amount of hot glue to the back of the gem's card stock setting and adhere it to the center of the blue satin ribbon, with the longer dimension of the gem crossing the width of the ribbon. Cool completely before wearing. Length of the ribbon is sufficient to circle a child's head and tie a bow at the nape of the neck.

ALADDIN'S FEZ

STEP 1 If your circular plastic storage container has a lip on the edge, remove it with scissors or kitchen shears.

STEP 2 Apply a line of hot glue from the container base to the edge. Center the short end of the red felt rectangle so that there is extra felt hanging over the base and the lip, and adhere. Apply another line of hot glue about an inch away from the first and secure the felt. Continue applying lines of hot glue at 1-inch intervals, pulling firmly to avoid ripples and puckering as you go.

STEP 3 Once the felt is wrapped completely around, glue the underside of the end of the piece of felt to the top of the front edge. Trim with scissors, perpendicular to the base, removing any excess past the overlap. Do not cut the overhang on the width.

STEP 4 Working in small increments, apply lines of hot glue, each about an inch long, parallel to the edge, just inside the lip of the container. Tuck in the overhanging felt so it adheres.

STEP 5 Again, working in small increments, apply hot glue to the base of the container and fold the excess felt up and over so it adheres to the base (which will be the top of the hat). Where it puckers, trim the excess so it lies flat.

STEP 6 Apply a few circles of hot glue on the base of the container, over the felt that has been folded up over the edges, and adhere the red felt circle.

STEP 7 About ¼ inch from the lip of the hat, glue on the metallic gold wavy trim all the way around the hat.

STEP 8 Tie a double knot about ½ inch from each end of the metallic gold elastic cord (length of the cord can be adjusted depending on the size of the child's head). Apply hot glue to one knot and the remaining ½ inch of cord beyond the knot and adhere to the inside of one side of the hat. Glue the other end of the cord in the same fashion to the opposite inside wall of the hat. Cool completely before wearing.

DIAMOND IN THE ROUGH ROCK CANDY

MAKES 6 FAVORS

MATERIALS

- MAGIC LAMP TEMPLATE (P. 166)
- 1 (8½ IN BY 11 IN) SHEET YELLOW CARD STOCK
- 6 (8 IN) LENGTHS OF YELLOW YARN
- 6 STICKS OF ROCK CANDY IN A VARIETY OF JEWEL TONES
- FAUX GEMS (OPTIONAL)
- VASE OR BOWL (OPTIONAL)

TOOLS:

- SCISSORS
- PENCIL
- ULTRA FINE POINT BLACK PERMANENT MARKER

> NOTE ➤ The materials can be scaled up for the number of guests invited to your party.

The Cave of Wonders will only allow a special person—a "diamond in the rough"—to enter its treasure-filled trove. Sticks of jewel-colored rock candy create a sparkly centerpiece when displayed in a bowl of faux gems, and then each stick—labeled with a magic lamp–shaped name tag—can be handed out as a favor at the end of the party.

INSTRUCTIONS

STEP 1 Using the Magic Lamp template on page 166, make a photocopy enlarging it 200 percent. Carefully cut out the shape—this will be your master template. Use a pencil to trace the lamp onto the yellow card stock six times. Carefully cut out the card stock lamps, including the holes in the handles.

STEP 2 Use a black marker to write each child's name across the center of each lamp.

STEP 3 Cut an 8-inch piece of yellow yarn for each name tag. Find the center of the piece of yarn and tie a cow-hitch knot around the end of a rock candy stick. Thread one of the loose ends of yarn through the handle of a card stock lamp. Now line up both loose ends and, treating them as one piece of yarn, tie an overhand knot about ½ inch from the ends.

STEP 4 Once all sticks have been labeled with name tags, display in a colorful vase or wide glass bowl to create a centerpiece. As guests depart, give each child his or her stick of rock candy to take home as a favor.

MUSICAL MAGIC CARPETS

MAKES 1 CARPET

MATERIALS

- 1 (12 IN BY 18 IN) FELT RECTANGLE IN A BRIGHT COLOR
- 1 (9 IN BY 12 IN) FELT RECTANGLE IN CONTRASTING BRIGHT COLOR
- 1 (38 IN) LENGTH METALLIC GOLD WAVY TRIM
- LARGE FAUX GEMS OR RHINESTONES IN A VARIETY OF SHAPES AND COLORS
- 1 (2 IN SQUARE) SHEET BLACK CARD STOCK
- 1 (80 IN) LENGTH YELLOW YARN

TOOLS:
- SCISSORS
- HOT GLUE GUN

NOTE The materials can be scaled up for the number of guests invited to your party.

Aladdin's trusty magic flying carpet is always there to get him out of precarious situations. In this update of Musical Chairs, magic carpets are used in place of chairs, with one removed after each round. Once you've made the tasseled and jeweled felt carpets, just queue up the *Aladdin* soundtrack on your stereo and get ready to play!

INSTRUCTIONS

STEP 1 Place the larger felt rectangle on your work surface. Position the smaller rectangle so it's centered on the larger rectangle and then adhere with hot glue.

STEP 2 Cut two pieces of metallic gold wavy trim measuring 11 inches long and 2 pieces measuring 8 inches long. Adhering with hot glue, position the trim on top of the smaller rectangle—11-inch pieces along the 12-inch sides, and 8-inch pieces along the 9-inch sides—about ¼ inch from the edges. The trim should meet in the corners.

STEP 3 Decorate the carpet with a variety of faux gems or rhinestones in different shapes and colors, adhered with hot glue. If placing gems in the corners of the carpet, make sure to leave at least ½ inch of felt so there will be room to glue on the tassels.

STEP 4 To make the tassels, hold the card stock square in one hand and use the other hand to wrap the yellow yarn around it five times.

Cut the yarn tail. Cut another piece of yarn about 4 inches long. Thread it underneath the loops on the card stock square and then tie it around the wraps to secure them. Slide the loops off the card stock. Cut another piece of yarn about 6 inches long. Wrap five times around the loops (including the yarn that was used to secure them) about a third of the way from the top of the loops. Tie a knot and pull tight. Snip off the excess so the strands of the tassel are roughly the same length, and snip open the bottoms of the loops so the strands of the tassel will hang loose. Create four tassels for each carpet.

STEP 5 Apply a small amount of hot glue to the knotted side of each tassel and adhere in the corners of the carpet. Cool completely before using.

HOW TO PLAY

When it's time to play, arrange the carpets on the floor in a circle. Instruct the children to walk around the perimeter of the carpets as the music plays. Once the music stops, each child must sit cross-legged on a carpet. After the first round, remove one carpet. When the music stops, the child left standing must leave the game. Continue removing one carpet each round until there is a winner.

BLUE GENIE PUNCH

MAKES 1 JAR

MATERIALS

- GENIE PUNCH TEMPLATE (P. 166)
- 1 (17½ OZ) GLASS MASON JAR (FREE OF EMBOSSING AND COMPLETELY BLANK ON AT LEAST 1 SIDE)
- POWDERED BLUE DRINK MIX
- WATER
- TRACING PAPER (OPTIONAL)

TOOLS:

- SCISSORS
- TRANSPARENT TAPE
- MEDIUM POINT WHITE PAINT MARKER
- MEDIUM POINT BLACK PAINT MARKER

NOTE → The materials can be scaled up for the number of guests invited to your party.

Despite having "phenomenal cosmic powers," the Genie would much rather give up his "itty-bitty living space" and be free. Perhaps a little roomier than the lamp, these Genie Punch jars don his unforgettable face. Any drink would work here, but the blue punch gives these a magical touch. For a low-sugar version, a blue reduced-calorie sports drink can be substituted for the powdered drink mix. The jars can double as favors for an added bonus.

INSTRUCTIONS

STEP 1 Using the Genie Punch template on page 166, make a photocopy or trace the template onto a piece of tracing paper. Then cut out Genie's face—this will be your master template. Place the paper inside the smooth side of the Mason jar with the image facing out and secure with tape.

STEP 2 With the white paint marker, using the image on the inside of the glass as a guide, draw the whites of Genie's eyes and his teeth on the outside of the glass. Let dry.

STEP 3 With the black paint marker, trace the rest of Genie's face on the outside of the glass. Let dry.

STEP 4 Remove the template and tape from the inside of the Mason jar and repeat with remaining jars.

STEP 5 Once all jars are decorated and dry, mix up a batch of blue punch according to the package instructions. You will need 16 ounces (2 cups) of punch to fill each Mason jar, so plan accordingly. It's always a good idea to have extra punch on hand for refills. Chill until ready to serve.

ANIMALS OF AGRABAH PITA CHIPS AND HUMMUS

**MAKES 16 (4 IN) ANIMAL CHIPS,
PLUS 80 (2 IN) TRIANGULAR CHIPS**

INGREDIENTS

- 4 (6 IN) WHOLE-WHEAT PITAS
- ½ CUP OLIVE OIL
- GARLIC POWDER, TO TASTE
- SALT, TO TASTE
- FRESHLY GROUND BLACK PEPPER, TO TASTE
- FAVORITE HUMMUS RECIPE
- BABY CARROTS
- CELERY STICKS

TOOLS:

- SMALL SERRATED KNIFE
- CUTTING BOARD
- 4-IN ANIMAL COOKIE CUTTERS
- SMALL BOWL
- NONSTICK BAKING SHEETS

In order to impress Princess Jasmine, Aladdin, posing as Prince Ali, makes a grand entrance in Agrabah riding an elephant, flanked by a myriad of animals, from monkeys to camels. All you need are a few different animal-shaped cookie cutters—elephants, tigers, giraffes, camels, lions, and monkeys are good choices—to bring the wildlife of Agrabah to your child's party. Serve this pita-chip menagerie with homemade hummus, carrots, and celery sticks for a healthy snack.

INSTRUCTIONS

STEP 1
Preheat oven to 400°F. Use a serrated knife to cut along the seam of each pita and split it into two circular halves. Lay each circular half on a cutting board and use cookie cutters to cut the pita into animal-shaped chips. You should be able to cut two 4-inch animals out of each pita half. Cut the scraps into 2-inch triangles.

STEP 2
In a small bowl, whisk together the olive oil, garlic powder, salt, and pepper. Adjust seasoning to taste. Place the pita chips on nonstick baking sheets and brush lightly with the olive oil mixture. Bake for 3 to 5 minutes, or until edges are golden brown. Watch through the oven door—they brown quickly! Cool completely.

STEP 3
Prepare your favorite hummus recipe. Serve with the freshly baked chips, baby carrots, and celery sticks.

ABU'S CARAMEL APPLES

MAKES 8 CARAMEL APPLES

INGREDIENTS

- 8 GRANNY SMITH APPLES
- 1 (24 OZ) PACKAGE WHITE, READY-TO-USE FONDANT
- 1 (24 OZ) PACKAGE BLACK, READY-TO-USE FONDANT
- 8 VANILLA WAFER COOKIES
- 16 BANANA CHIPS
- 8 LARGE GUMDROPS
- 2 (14 OZ) PACKAGES INDIVIDUALLY WRAPPED CARAMELS
- 4 TBSP MILK
- POWDERED SUGAR, FOR ROLLING
- 1 (4¼ OZ) TUBE OF BLACK FROSTING, FITTED WITH WRITING TIP

TOOLS:

- BAKING SHEET
- PARCHMENT PAPER
- 8 PAPER CRAFT STICKS
- ROLLING PIN
- 1 (1 IN) CIRCULAR COOKIE OR FONDANT CUTTER
- 1 (½ IN) CIRCULAR COOKIE OR FONDANT CUTTER
- PARING KNIFE (OPTIONAL)
- CAP OF A FINE-TIP MARKER (OPTIONAL)

Every Disney hero needs at least one loyal—and comical—sidekick, and Abu is Aladdin's. This resourceful monkey helps Aladdin steal an apple from the marketplace. These playful caramel apples end your party on a sweet note.

INSTRUCTIONS

STEP 1   Cover a baking sheet with a piece of parchment paper. Twist off the stem of each apple and insert one end of a paper craft stick, pushing it in about 1 inch.

STEP 2   Roll out white fondant to a thickness of ⅛ inch. If it gets too sticky, sprinkle with powdered sugar. Using the 1-inch cookie or fondant cutter, cut two circles to make the eyes.

STEP 3   Roll out black fondant to a thickness of ⅛ inch, sprinkling with powdered sugar if it gets sticky. Using the ½-inch fondant or cookie cutter (or a sharp paring knife), cut two circles to make the irises. Cut two additional circles, about ¼ inch in diameter, to make the nostrils. (The cap of a fine-tip marker works well for this.) Brush the backs of the irises with a tiny bit of water and adhere to the whites of the eyes. Gently press the nostrils onto the vanilla wafer cookie, close together, near one edge.

STEP 4   Select banana chips that are similar in size. Set aside with gumdrops.

STEP 5 Unwrap the caramels and place in a heatproof bowl. Add the milk and microwave at 30-second intervals, stirring between each interval, until completely melted.

STEP 6 Dip each apple in the melted caramel, rolling back and forth and spooning caramel over the top until covered. Place on parchment-lined baking sheet.

STEP 7 Immediately adhere the vanilla wafer cookie muzzle in the bottom-center area of the face (the caramel will set quickly). Place the eyes just above the muzzle, about ¼ inch apart. Press a large gumdrop atop the front of the apple for Abu's fez, and stick a banana chip into each side for ears. Lastly, use the black icing with the writing tip to draw a smile on the muzzle. Place entire tray in refrigerator and chill until ready to serve.

JAFAR'S GIFT!

GAME FOR 5–25 GUESTS

- 1 GIFT OF YOUR CHOOSING
- A LOT OF OLD NEWSPAPERS
- GIFT WRAPPING PAPER
- TAPE
- RIBBONS AND GIFT DECORATIONS
- 5–25 ENTHUSIASTIC CHILDREN
- ANY KIND OF MUSIC

Believe it or not Jafar just loves birthdays! When he was a child growing up in the palace he invented a game for his 10th birthday, a game he thought only he could win! But Jaffar has always been too clever for his own good ... as you will find out playing Jaffar's Gift!

INSTRUCTIONS

STEP 1 Create a big gift with many, many layers. Start with the actual reward or gift. It can be anything and can be any size. This will, however, determine the eventual size of the final gift.

STEP 2 When the first gift is done add another layer of paper, alternating with plain newspaper and genuine gift wrappings. The more layers the better. The more tape the better. This should be a really difficult gift to open!

STEP 3 Gather the players in a tight circle and put the big gift in the middle. Decide who holds it first.

STEP 4 Start playing the music. Any kind will do, but the livelier the better.

STEP 5   While the music is playing the person holding the gift hands it over to the person on their left who then hands the gift to their left. And so on, while the music is playing.

STEP 6   Stop the music! At that instant, the person holding the gift can start to tear it apart! Just go for it!

STEP 7   The music starts again and the person in the ripping frenzy has to stop immediately and hand it over to the person on their left.

STEP 8   And on it goes. The music stops again, the gift gets torn assunder, the music starts and the gift is passed on.

STEP 9   The person who gets through the final layer wins the game and gets to keep Jafar's Gift! Enjoy!

WHO'S UNDER THE BLANKET?

GAME FOR 10–25 GUESTS

MATERIALS

♥ 1 BLANKET

Although Aladdin's Magic Carpet would take offense with being called a blanket, he would really love this fun and exciting game.

INSTRUCTIONS

STEP 1 Gather the players in a tight circle. The one in charge selects one player and sends him out of the room.

STEP 2 A second player is selected, put into the center of the circle and covered with a blanket.

STEP 3 All the other players now sing out loud "Who's under the blanket".

STEP 4 The player who was sent out of the room comes inside and tries to guess who's under the blanket by saying the name of the one he thinks is there.

STEP 5 If he gets it right the player under the blanket goes out of the room. The guesser gets to choose who goes next under the blanket.

TIP Rotate the players in the circle for more difficulty.
Player gets 3 tries to guess a name. If he fails he sits down with the group and the one under the blanket leaves the room.

PRINCESS
PARTY

Eleven Disney princesses have been coronated, starting with Snow White in 1937. Ranging from a redheaded mermaid to a Chinese warrior, the princesses could not be more different. And yet they possess important common qualities that make them role models for children all over the world. Each Disney Princess is kind and compassionate and possesses the courage to follow her dreams.

Short of sending a palace messenger to the home of each guest, the best way to announce an upcoming Disney Princess birthday party is by sending out Cinderella's Slipper Invitations. Once the representatives of the court have gathered in the ballroom—decorated with Rapunzel's Golden Braid Garlands—they can create Tiana's Princess Party Tiaras as well as Fairy Godmother Wands. The menu for the royal buffet includes Belle's French Baguette Sandwiches, Ariel's Follow-Your-Heart Fruit Skewers, and Princess Aurora's Tiara Cake.

CINDERELLA'S GLASS SLIPPER INVITATIONS

MAKES 2 INVITATIONS

MATERIALS

Cinderella's glass slipper is all that remains after her beautiful ball gown and pumpkin coach transform when the stroke of midnight breaks the spell. Since the slipper is what brings the grand duke to her doorstep, it makes for the perfect invitation to a princess party.

- ❤ CINDERELLA GLASS SLIPPER INVITATION TEMPLATE (P. 166)
- ❤ 1 (9 IN BY 12 IN) SHEET LIGHT BLUE HEAVYWEIGHT CRAFT PAPER
- ❤ 1 (9 IN BY 12 IN) SHEET DECORATIVE WHITE, OFF-WHITE, OR SPARKLY HEAVYWEIGHT CRAFT PAPER
- ❤ GLITTER GLUE
- ❤ ENVELOPES (OPTIONAL)

TOOLS:
- ❤ PENCIL
- ❤ TRACING PAPER
- ❤ SCISSORS
- ❤ FINE POINT BLACK PEN
- ❤ PERMANENT MARKER
- ❤ GLUE STICK
- ❤ SMALL, STIFF PAINTBRUSH

INSTRUCTIONS

STEP 1 Using the Cinderella Glass Slipper Invitation template on page 166, make a photocopy or trace the template onto a piece of tracing paper. Carefully cut out both shapes—this will be your master template.

STEP 2 Trace the slipper backing piece twice onto light blue heavyweight craft paper and the glass slipper piece twice onto the decorative white or sparkly white craft paper. Cut out both tracings.

STEP 3 With the black marker, write the party particulars on the back of each slipper.

NOTE The materials can be scaled up for the number of guests invited to your party.

STEP 4 Use the glue stick to apply adhesive to the back of the white slipper piece. Adhere to the front of the blue backing piece so that the rear edges of the heels line up.

STEP 5 Use a paintbrush to apply glitter glue to the front of the slipper. Let it dry completely and place in envelopes, if using.

TIANA'S PRINCESS PARTY TIARA

MAKES 2 TIARAS

MATERIALS

- TIANA'S PRINCESS PARTY TIARA TEMPLATE (P. 166)
- 3 (9 IN BY 12 IN) SHEETS TEXTURED DECORATIVE WHITE CRAFT PAPER*
- 3 (8½ IN BY 11 IN) SHEETS WHITE CARD STOCK (OPTIONAL)
- 4 BOBBY PINS
- SELF-ADHESIVE FAUX GEMS AND/OR OTHER DECORATIVE DETAILS

TOOLS:
- SCISSORS
- PENCIL
- GLUE STICK
- RULER (OPTIONAL)
- PUSHPIN

NOTE → The materials can be scaled up for the number of guests invited to your party.

* If the craft paper won't be stiff enough to hold its shape once the gems have been adhered, glue it to a sheet of white card stock before cutting out the tiara pieces.

An ambitious aspiring New Orleans restaurateur, Tiana doesn't have time for distractions such as love—that is, until she kisses a frog and falls for Prince Naveen. Little royals will love decorating—and wearing—the tiara that Tiana wears to her friend Charlotte's masquerade ball.

INSTRUCTIONS

STEP 1 Using Tiana's Princess Party Tiara template on page 166, make a photocopy enlarging it 200 percent. Carefully cut out the shapes—this will be your master template.

STEP 2 Trace the center and M-shaped pieces onto the decorative craft paper (it may be easier to do this on the non-textured side). Then trace the base piece onto the decorative paper twice (once for the backing, and once for the face of the tiara). Cut out all the tracings.

STEP 3 To assemble the tiara, use a glue stick to apply adhesive to the lower part of the M-shaped piece. Position the piece centered atop the base backing (you may want to use a ruler to find the exact center point), making sure that the straight bottom edges of the legs are flush with the bottom edge of the backing. Press lightly to adhere.

STEP 4 Glue the inverted V-shaped center point to the base in the same manner.

STEP 5   Finally, glue the face of the base atop the backing, sandwiching the bottoms of the point pieces between them.

STEP 6   Use the pushpin to poke a small hole near each end of the tiara base. Then slip a bobby pin through each hole so the tiara will be ready to be secured in the wearer's hair.

STEP 7   At the party, let each guest decorate a tiara with plenty of faux gems and other details.

RAPUNZEL'S GOLDEN BRAID GARLAND

MAKES 1 (72-INCH) GARLAND

MATERIALS

- 1 LARGE SKEIN OF YELLOW YARN (COTTON YARN WORKS WELL)
- ASSORTED DECORATIVE FABRIC FLOWERS

TOOLS:
- YARD STICK OR MEASURING TAPE
- SCISSORS
- LOW-TEMPERATURE HOT GLUE GUN

Rapunzel's yards of glorious golden hair become a bit of a nuisance—that is when not being used as a lasso, whip, or belaying rope. So she is delighted when the children of the kingdom weave her locks into a thick, flowered braid. Pretty and fun to make, these garlands are ideal decorations for a Disney Princess party.

INSTRUCTIONS

STEP 1 Begin by making two long braids. For each one, cut nine 5-yard lengths of yarn. Gather them in a long hank and fold in half. Use a 6-inch piece of yarn to bind the hank 1½ inches below the fold to form a small loop.

STEP 2 Slip the loop over a small hook or cabinet knob to make an anchor for the braiding process. Then divide the strands into three groups of six, and braid the groups, being careful not to tangle them (no pun intended). When you reach the end, bind it tightly with another 6-inch piece of yarn.

STEP 3 Cut twenty-four 4-yard lengths of yarn, gather them in a hank and fold in half. Use a 6-inch piece of yarn to bind the hank 1½ inches below the fold to form a loop. Do not braid this yarn.

STEP 4 Tie the two braids and the loose hank together with a 6-inch piece of yarn threaded through all three of the top loops. Then, very loosely, wind the two braids around the loose strands. Use a 12-inch length of yarn to tightly bind the three sections together a few inches from the bottom.

STEP 5 Use 4-inch lengths of yarn to loosely tie the three sections together every 4 inches or so between the top loops and the bottom binding. Trim the ends of all the ties close to the knots.

STEP 6 Finally, decorate the garland by using hot glue to adhere assorted fabric flowers onto the yarn.

STEP 7 To double the length of the garland, make a second one as you did the first. Then use an additional strand of yarn to tie the two looped ends together.

FAIRY GODMOTHER WANDS

MAKES 1 WAND

MATERIALS

- 1 (12 IN) BAMBOO DOWEL
- WHITE ACRYLIC CRAFT PAINT
- GLITTER GLUE
- 1 (20 IN) BLUE SHIMMERY RIBBON, ¼ IN TO ⅜ IN WIDE
- 1 (20 IN) WHITE SHIMMERY RIBBON, ¼ IN TO ⅜ IN WIDE
- 2 (1½ IN WIDE) ADHESIVE SPARKLY WHITE OR BLUE CRAFT FOAM STARS*
- 1 (9 IN BY 12 IN) SHEET SPARKLY CRAFT PAPER (OPTIONAL)

TOOLS:

- CRAFT SPONGE
- SMALL PAINTBRUSH
- RULER
- TACKY GLUE (OPTIONAL)

NOTE → The materials can be scaled up for the number of guests invited to your party.

* As an alternative to craft foam stars, you can cut pairs of stars out of sparkly craft paper and then stick them together using tacky glue.

Cinderella's Fairy Godmother is definitely well intentioned, but perhaps a bit absent-minded. After all, she can't find her magic wand when she first appears in the garden. But when she does find it—and remembers the magic words—she conjures a pumpkin coach, Cinderella's glittering gown, and glass slippers to match. To make wands just like the Fairy Godmother's, all you need is a few simple materials and "Bibbidi Babbidi Boo!" The dowel rods used as the base of the wands can be found in the cake-decorating section of craft stores.

INSTRUCTIONS

STEP 1 First, use the craft sponge and white acrylic paint to paint the dowel white. Once the paint has dried, use a small paintbrush to apply glitter glue along the top third of each wand. Set aside to dry completely. (Tip: you can set them upright in a jar to let them dry.)

STEP 2 While the dowel is drying, cut 20-inch lengths of both the blue and the white ribbon (one length of each color for each wand). After the dowel is dry, tie a pair of ribbons (one white, one blue) at roughly their center point, around the top of a wand (about ½ inch from the end). Then tie an overhand knot in the end of each strand.

STEP 3 To complete the wand, stick a pair of craft foam stars together—adhesive sides facing each other—sandwiching the top of the dowel between them. If needed, use a little tacky glue to make sure they hold.

ARIEL'S FOLLOW-YOUR-HEART FRUIT SKEWERS

MAKES 24 FRUIT SKEWERS

INGREDIENTS

- 1 SMALL SEEDLESS WATERMELON
- 1 MEDIUM/LARGE CANTALOUPE
- 1 MEDIUM/LARGE HONEYDEW MELON
- 1 (5 OZ TO 6 OZ) CUP LEMON-FLAVORED YOGURT (GREEK OR REGULAR)

TOOLS:

- BUTCHER OR CHEF'S KNIFE
- 1 (1½ IN) HEART-SHAPED COOKIE OR FONDANT CUTTER
- TRAY
- PAPER TOWELS
- 24 (12 IN) WOOD OR BAMBOO SKEWERS
- PLATTER

From the moment Ariel first sees Eric aboard his ship, the little mermaid knows that she wants to be part of his world. So despite her father's rules, she saves the prince from drowning and follows her heart, trading her voice for a chance to be human. Comprised of three fruit hearts—one each of watermelon, cantaloupe, and honeydew melon—these skewers are pretty, festive, and fit for a princess.

INSTRUCTIONS

STEP 1 Beginning with the watermelon, slice melon in half lengthwise. Cut each half into slices approximately ½ inch thick. Using the heart-shaped cookie or fondant cutter, cut out twenty-four watermelon hearts. Place on a tray lined with paper towel and refrigerate until ready to use.

STEP 2 Repeat step 1 with the cantaloupe and honeydew melon. The leftover melon pieces can be used later in a fruit salad or a smoothie.

STEP 3 To assemble, thread a honeydew heart onto a skewer. The skewer should go through the widest part of the heart so that the shape faces up when displayed. Follow with a cantaloupe heart, and finish with a watermelon heart. Repeat with remaining skewers. Arrange finished skewers on a platter and serve with lemon-flavored yogurt for dipping.

BELLE'S BAGUETTE PARTY SANDWICHES

MAKES 8 SANDWICHES

INGREDIENTS

- 8 RADISHES, WASHED
- 2 (12 IN) BAGUETTES
- MAYONNAISE
- MUSTARD
- 16 SLICES HAM
- 16 SLICES CHEESE
- VEGGIE CREAM CHEESE (OPTIONAL)
- SLICED VEGETABLES (OPTIONAL)

TOOLS:

- PARING KNIFE
- BOWL OR PLASTIC CONTAINER
- SERRATED KNIFE
- PAPER TOWELS
- TOOTHPICKS

Brainy, beautiful, and book-obsessed, Belle might be misunderstood by the inhabitants of her provincial French town, but that doesn't stop her from being outgoing and kind to everyone she meets. With slices of French baguette as their foundation, these sandwiches can be filled with any combination of sliced meat, cheese, and veggies that the birthday kid prefers. Carved radish roses add an enchanting garnish!

INSTRUCTIONS

STEP 1 To make each radish rose, begin by using a sharp paring knife to slice a thin portion off the top and bottom of the radish. Create the outer circle of petals by making five vertical cuts in the shape of a pentagon around the perimeter of the radish. Make each cut just shy of the widest part of the radish, and slice down about three quarters of the way to the base. Don't worry if your cuts overlap slightly—it will just make the petals look more elaborate.

STEP 2 Just inside the five outer petals, make a second round of five cuts, slicing each of the points of the pentagon created in step 1.

STEP 3 Make a third layer of petals by repeating the process described in step 2.

STEP 4   Finally, carve the center of the rose by making three shallow cuts in the shape of a small triangle.

STEP 5   Place carved radish roses in a bowl or plastic container, fill with cold water, and chill until ready to display. This will help the petals to open up. For the best results, carve the radish roses the day before the party or at least several hours beforehand.

STEP 6   To make the sandwiches, use a serrated knife to cut each baguette into four 3-inch segments. Then slice each segment in half horizontally.

STEP 7   Spread the top half of each segment with either mayonnaise or mustard, and layer two slices of ham and cheese on each of the bottom halves. Replace the top halves. For a vegetarian version, the sandwiches can be made with sliced vegetables and veggie cream cheese.

STEP 8   Just before serving, remove the radish roses from refrigerator, drain, and pat dry with paper towels. Insert a toothpick halfway into the bottom of each radish rose, and then insert the other end of the toothpick into the top of a prepared sandwich so the rose sits on top. Serve and enjoy!

PRINCESS AURORA'S TIARA CAKE

MAKES 1 (2 LAYER) 8 IN OR 9 IN ROUND CAKE

INGREDIENTS

- PRINCESS AURORA TIARA CAKE TEMPLATE (P. 166)

INGREDIENTS:

- 1 (1 LB) PACKAGE READY-TO-USE GUM PASTE
- PINK OR RED FOOD COLORING
- GOLD FOOD COLORING SPRAY
- EDIBLE GOLD DUST
- FAVORITE RECIPE FOR A 2-LAYER (8 IN OR 9 IN) ROUND CAKE, PREPARED AND FROSTED
- PREPARED FONDANT (OPTIONAL)
- HEART-SHAPED CAKE-DECORATING CANDIES (OPTIONAL)

TOOLS:

- SCISSORS
- WAX PAPER
- ROLLING PIN
- PARING KNIFE
- LARGE (42 OZ) CARDBOARD OATMEAL CANISTER OR SIMILAR CONTAINER, ABOUT 5 IN IN DIAMETER
- 1 (¼ IN) HEART-SHAPED FONDANT CUTTER (OPTIONAL)
- SMALL, CLEAN PAINTBRUSH

Growing up in a forest cottage with the three fairies, Briar Rose is completely unaware that she is Princess Aurora. It isn't until her sixteenth birthday that she learns of her true identity—and receives a golden tiara. There is no sweeter ending to a princess party than this scrumptious cake, decorated with pink and red hearts, pink gum-paste roses, and a glittering gold tiara, just like Aurora's.

INSTRUCTIONS

STEP 1   Using the Princess Aurora Tiara Cake template on page 166, make a photocopy enlarging it 200 percent. Carefully cut out the shape—this will be your master template.

STEP 2   Place a large piece of wax paper on your work surface. Working with about two thirds of the gum paste (between 10 and 11 ounces), roll it out to a ¼-inch thickness. Place the tiara template on top of the gum paste and trace around it with a paring knife. Remove the excess gum paste and save for another project. If desired, use the heart-shaped fondant cutter to stamp partial impressions (do not cut all the way through the gum paste) just below each of the points of the tiara.

STEP 3 Lay the oatmeal canister on its side and cover with a piece of wax paper. Carefully drape the gum paste tiara over it so that the long end of the tiara is perpendicular to the length of the canister. Set aside and allow the gum paste to harden until the tiara will hold its curved shape when set upright. This may take a few hours depending on the temperature and humidity. Once the tiara has stiffened, set upright on its curved bottom edge and allow it to harden completely, about one to two days.

STEP 4 To make the roses, separate out a piece of gum paste roughly the size of your palm. Add red or pink food coloring and knead until gum paste is uniform in color and the shade of pink you desire. Roll out to ¼-inch thickness. Use the circular fondant cutter to cut out ten circles. Remove excess and save for another project.

STEP 5 Place five gum-paste circles in a line, overlapping the edges slightly. Apply a tiny drop of water underneath each edge and press gently to adhere. Beginning at one end, roll up the line of circles, rolling the first circle tightly and then rolling the remaining circles more loosely. Pinch one end of the finished roll to create the base of the flower, and then gently separate and curl the petals. Set aside to stiffen. Repeat with the second group of five circles.

STEP 6 Once the gum paste tiara has hardened completely, spritz the front side of it with gold food coloring spray. After the spray has dried, brush the front side of the tiara with edible gold dust for extra shimmer.

STEP 7 Prepare your favorite recipe for a 2-layer 8- or 9-inch round cake. Once frosted in desired icing (an even layer of white buttercream works well), set the tiara and the roses on top of the cake. (Tip: if the frosting is overly fluffy or creamy, you can roll out a portion of fondant, and cut an 8- or 9-inch circle to fit the top of the cake. It will prevent the tiara and roses from sinking down into the frosting.) If desired, decorate the circumference of the cake with candy hearts.

THE JEWEL QUEST!

GAME FOR 5–25 GUESTS

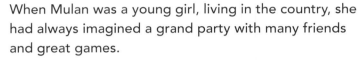

MATERIALS

- 5 DIFFERENT COLOR ELASTIC ARM BANDS
  5 FOR EACH GUEST

When Mulan was a young girl, living in the country, she had always imagined a grand party with many friends and great games.
The Jewel Quest is one of the games she invented.

INSTRUCTIONS

STEP 1 When greeting your guests at the party you give them five different colored arm jewels with the greeting: "Please receive these precious jewels and guard them well!"

STEP 2 You then give each guest the 2 words they cannot say throughout the whole party. Choose words that are often used and easy to remember, like "no", "maybe" or "red".

STEP 3 All the party guests now have the task of making the other guests say those forbidden words.

STEP 4 If a party guest succeeds in getting another to say a forbidden word she gets a jewel from that guest.

STEP 5 This game goes on for the duration of the party. The guest with the most jewels in the end wins.

NOTE → If a guest has lost all her colored jewels she need not despair. She can still play the game and try to win more jewels!

DANCE OF ACES

GAME FOR 5–25 GUESTS

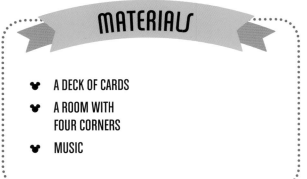

MATERIALS

- A DECK OF CARDS
- A ROOM WITH FOUR CORNERS
- MUSIC

If there is one thing princess Merida loves it's a great dance! Join her in the Dance of Aces where you will choose your own specific Ace. But beware! All is not as it seems.

INSTRUCTIONS

Four aces, one of each kind, are put into the four corners of the room.

The Master of Ceremonies turns on the music and everyone dances to their hearts desire.

After a while the music is turned off and everyone goes to the Ace of their choosing.

The MC then draws a card from the deck and shows it. Those who picked the corner with the corresponding sort are out of the dance. For instance if a spade is drawn, those in the corner of the ace of spades are out.

The MC turns the music back on and the dance begins again. The game is over when there is one dancer left. He gets to be the MC in the next dance.

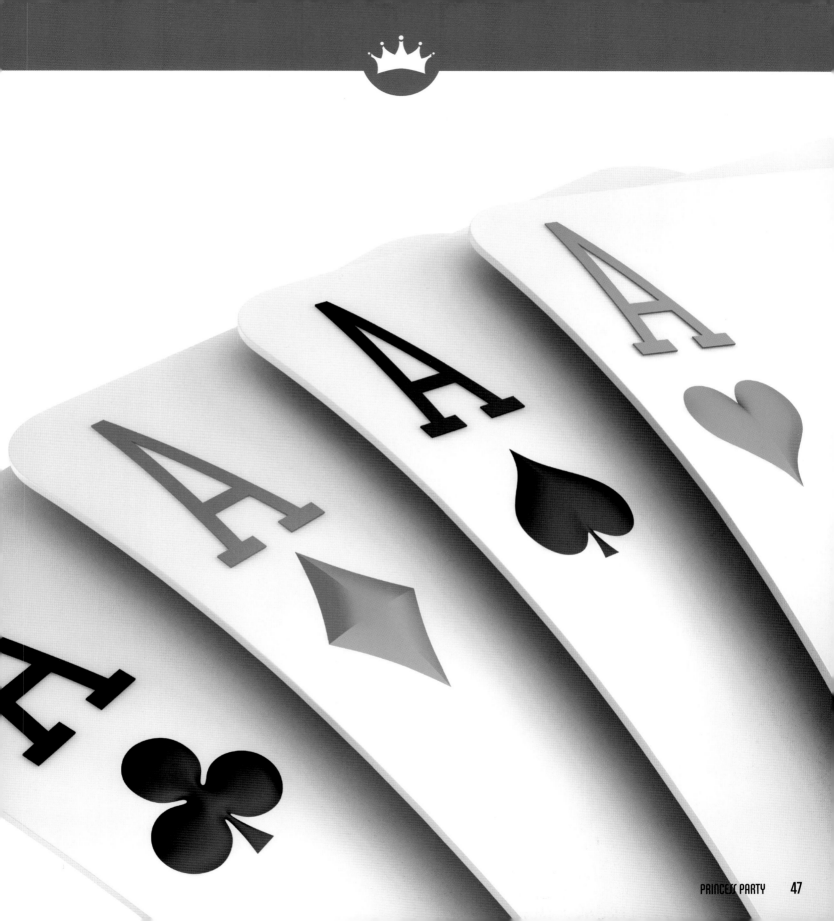

TOY STORY
PARTY

The first ever all computer-animated feature, *Toy Story* changed the face of family entertainment—to infinity and beyond!—when it was released in 1995. The story centers on Woody, a cowboy toy, who is struck with jealousy when he is replaced as Andy's favorite toy by a new birthday present: Buzz Lightyear. The film's wild popularity has led to the production of two sequels: *Toy Story 2* (1999) and *Toy Story 3* (2010), which introduced new toys, set records at the box office, and moved audiences to laugh and cry.

Once you've set a date for your child's *Toy Story* party, round up the cowboys and cowgirls by sending them Woody's Cowboy Vest Invitations. Before the rodeo begins, decorate the ranch with the Three-Eyed Aliens Garland, and then get ready to play Pass the Pig! When it's time for grub, chow down on Cheesy Wheezys and Woody's Sheriff Badge Sandwiches. Finish with the intergalactic Buzz Lightyear cake and bid little cowpokes farewell with Woody's Cowboy Boot Favors.

WOODY'S COWBOY VEST INVITATION

MAKES 3 INVITATIONS

MATERIALS

- WOODY'S COWBOY VEST INVITATION TEMPLATE (P. 170)
- BLACK ACRYLIC CRAFT PAINT
- 1 (8½ IN BY 11 IN) SHEET WHITE CARD STOCK (WILL MAKE 3 INVITES)
- 1 (8½ IN BY 11 IN) SHEET YELLOW CARD STOCK (WILL MAKE 4 INVITES)
- 1 (4 IN SQUARE) GOLD-FOIL CRAFT PAPER (WILL MAKE 9 INVITES)
- 6 (½ IN) BUTTONS
- ENVELOPES (OPTIONAL)

TOOLS:

- SCISSORS
- PENCIL
- SYNTHETIC CRAFT SPONGE
- ULTRA FINE POINT BLACK PERMANENT MARKER
- GLUE SEALER (SUCH AS MOD PODGE®)
- SMALL FOAM BRUSH
- RULER
- ULTRA FINE POINT RED PERMANENT MARKER
- TACKY GLUE

NOTE → The materials can be scaled up for the number of guests invited to your party.

Woody, a cowboy pull-string doll, is Andy's favorite toy—that is, until Andy receives a Buzz Lightyear action figure for his birthday. At first, Woody is jealous of the space ranger, but after a dangerous adventure in the world outside of Andy's room, the two toys become friends. Impart a charming "Howdy, pardner!" to your child's friends by sending out these rootin' tootin' invites, complete with sheriff's badges.

INSTRUCTIONS

STEP 1 Using the Woody's Cowboy Vest Invitation template on page 170, make a photocopy enlarging 200 percent. Carefully cut out all of the shapes—this will be your master template.

STEP 2 Trace the vest onto a sheet of white card stock and cut it out.

STEP 3 Trace the shirt onto a sheet of yellow card stock and cut it out.

STEP 4 Trace the star onto a piece of gold craft paper and cut it out.

STEP 5 Cut a small piece of craft sponge, dip it in the black acrylic paint, and use it to create a cowhide pattern on one side of the white vest, making sure to leave a ¼-inch border free of paint along the sides and curved bottom edge. Set aside to dry.

STEP 6 Once the paint has dried, use the ultra fine point black permanent marker to draw a border on the sides and bottom of the white vest. Begin on one side of the straight top edge, about ¼ inch from the side edge, and follow the curve down that side, across the bottom, and up the other side.

STEP 7 Create a rope pattern in the border by drawing diagonal lines at ¼-inch intervals, between the line drawn in step 6 and the outside edge of the vest.

STEP 8 Use the foam brush to apply a coat of glue sealer over the front of the vest. Set aside to dry completely.

STEP 9 While the vest is drying, use the ruler and the ultra fine point red permanent marker to create a plaid pattern on the yellow shirt piece. First draw a series of vertical lines at ½-inch intervals across the span of the shirt piece. Then draw a series of horizontal lines at ½-inch intervals across the span of the shirt.

STEP 10 Once the vest is dry, turn it over so the blank white side is facing up. Place the yellow shirt piece in the center of the vest, top edge flush with the top edge of the vest, and then fold the sides of the vest up and over the sides of the shirt piece.

STEP 11 Write the party particulars on the inside of the vest flaps or on the back of the shirt piece.

STEP 12 Use tacky glue to adhere two buttons to the center of the shirt, positioning the first one about 1 inch down from the top edge of the shirt, and the second one ¾ inch below the first.

STEP 13 Apply a small amount of tacky glue to the back of the gold star and adhere it to the right side of the vest, about ½ inch from the top edge.

STEP 14 Place in envelopes, if using.

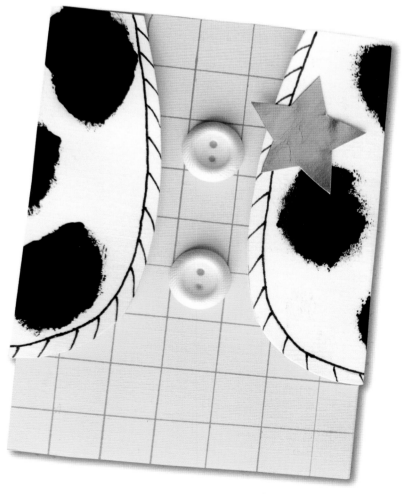

HAMM TABLETOP DECORATION & GAME

MAKES 1 CENTERPIECE

- 1 (6 IN BY 3 IN) STYROFOAM CONE
- 1 (8½ IN BY 11 IN) SHEET WHITE PAPER
- 1 (4 IN) SMOOTH, HARD FOAM BALL
- 1 (3 IN) SMOOTH, HARD FOAM BALL
- PINK ACRYLIC CRAFT PAINT
- 4 WINE CORKS
- 8 TOOTHPICKS
- 2 (⅝ IN) GOOGLY EYES
- 1 (9 IN BY 12 IN) SHEET BLACK CONSTRUCTION PAPER
- 1 (9 IN BY 12 IN) SHEET PINK FELT

TOOLS:

- SERRATED KNIFE
- SCISSORS
- ¾ IN SOFT PAINTBRUSH
- GLUE SEALER (SUCH AS MOD PODGE®)
- TACKY GLUE

Although Hamm, also known as the evil Dr. Porkchop, often occupies the role of the villain during Andy's playtime, this piggy bank is truly a softie at heart. He can serve as both a centerpiece and a game piece for Pass the Pig. It's just like Hot Potato—except "You've Got a Friend in Me" is playing and Hamm is the spud!

INSTRUCTIONS

STEP 1 Begin by creating Hamm's snout from the Styrofoam cone. Use a finely serrated knife to slice a portion of the center of the cone that measures about 1¾ inches long. The diameter of the larger end should be about 2¼ inches, and the diameter of the smaller end should be about 1¾ inches.

STEP 2 Wrap a piece of white paper around the outside of the snout and use a pencil to mark the dimensions. Unwrap the paper and cut out the resulting shape. Using the paintbrush, apply glue sealer to one side of the paper and adhere it to the outside of the snout so that the edges are flush and it wraps around completely. Then cut a circle of white paper 1¾ inches in diameter. Apply glue sealer to the paper circle and adhere it to the smaller end of the snout. If needed, apply one to two additional layers of glue sealer and paper so that the surface is as smooth as possible. Set aside to dry completely.

STEP 3 To create Hamm's body, set the 4-inch foam ball on your work surface and use the knife to cut a thin slice—between ⅜- and ½-inch thick—from one end of the sphere. This should create a flat circular surface on the sphere about 2¼ inches in diameter.

STEP 4 To prepare Hamm's head, set the 3-inch foam ball on your work surface and use the knife to cut a thin slice—between ⅜- and ½-inch thick—from one end of the sphere. Then cut a corresponding slice from the opposite end of the sphere. (To give the pig a bit more character, skew this cut slightly left of center.) There should now be two flat circular surfaces on opposite ends of the sphere, each about 2¼ inches in diameter.

STEP 5 Use the paintbrush to apply a coat of pink craft paint to all surfaces of Hamm's snout (created in steps 1 and 2), Hamm's body (created in step 3), and Hamm's head (created in step 4). Then paint the four wine corks. Allow the paint to dry.

STEP 6 Once the pieces have dried, apply a layer of tacky glue onto the flat circular surface on Hamm's body (the larger ball). Insert two toothpicks halfway into the glue-covered flat circular surface. Line up one of the flat ends of

Hamm's head (the smaller ball) with the glue-covered surface of the body. Push the head onto the protruding toothpicks and continue pushing until the flat surfaces are pressed together.

STEP 7 To attach the snout, apply a layer of tacky glue onto the remaining flat circular surface on Hamm's head (the smaller ball). Insert two toothpicks halfway into the glue-covered flat circular surface. Line up the larger end of Hamm's snout with the glue-covered surface of the head. Push the snout onto the protruding toothpicks and continue pushing until the flat surfaces are pressed together. Set aside to dry completely.

STEP 8 Once the body is dry, attach the legs by applying tacky glue onto one narrow end of each painted wine cork. Insert a toothpick halfway into the glue-covered end of each cork, and then press the toothpick into the body, positioning the legs so that they splay out. (It may take a bit of trial and error to get the legs positioned in such a way that they support the body without the head and snout weighing it down.) Allow the glue to dry.

STEP 9 When the glue is dry, apply another coat (or two) of pink acrylic paint to the entire pig.

STEP 10 To make Hamm's eyes, use scissors to cut open the googly eyes and remove the pupils. Apply a small amount of tacky glue to one side of each pupil and then adhere them to the pig's head, midway between the highest part of the head and the top edge of the snout, spaced about ⅝ inch apart. To make eyebrows, cut two small crescent shapes

to become a cup shape. Apply tacky glue to the back of the overlapped edges and adhere the ears to the highest part of Hamm's head, set just wider than his eyes. Once the glue is dry, use scissors to shape the tips of the ears as desired.

STEP 14 To make Hamm's nostrils, cut two teardrops of pink felt measuring ⅜ inch long by ¼ inch wide. Apply tacky glue to one side of each teardrop and adhere to the circular end of the pig's snout, ⅜ inch from the top edge of the snout and spaced ¼ inch apart.

STEP 15 To make Hamm's tail, cut a circle of pink felt measuring 1¼ inches in diameter. Cut the circle into a spiral. Apply tacky glue to the outer end of the spiral and adhere it to the center of the pig's rear end. Allow glue to dry completely before using as a tabletop decoration or game piece.

about ⅛ inch thick and ½ inch long from black craft paper. Glue one eyebrow about ⅛ inch above each pupil.

STEP 11 Create Hamm's hooves by cutting four circles of black craft paper measuring ⅝ inch in diameter. Cut off the bottom third of each circle and discard it. Apply tacky glue to one side of each hoof. Adhere one hoof at the base of each of Hamm's legs so the flat edge of each hoof is flush with the bottom of the leg and the hoof is facing the snout-end of the pig.

STEP 12 Brush the entire pig with one to two coats of glue sealer and allow it to dry completely.

STEP 13 Create Hamm's ears by cutting two circles of pink felt measuring ¾ inch in diameter. Make a snip in each ear, starting at the edge and cutting ¼ inch toward the center. Then overlap the snipped ends by ¼ inch, pulling them toward each other, causing the felt circle

HOW TO PLAY

When it's time to play "Pass the Pig," the party guests should sit in a circle. Play the song "You've Got a Friend in Me" from the *Toy Story* soundtrack and hand the pig to the birthday girl or boy. Instruct the children to pass the pig around the circle as the music plays, and then hit pause spontaneously. Whichever child is holding the pig when the music stops is eliminated from the game. Play proceeds in this fashion until one child is left and declared the winner. The pig can be awarded as a prize, or if additional rounds of the game are to be played, a small toy or treat can be given out to the winner of each round, with the pig being reserved for the finale.

THREE-EYED ALIENS GARLAND

MAKES 1 (31½-INCH) GARLAND

MATERIALS

- ❤ THREE-EYED ALIENS GARLAND TEMPLATE (P. 170)
- ❤ 1 (9 IN BY 12 IN) SHEET BRIGHT GREEN CRAFT PAPER (MAKES 9 ALIENS)
- ❤ 1 (9 IN BY 12 IN) SHEET BLACK CRAFT PAPER
- ❤ 27 WHITE PAPER HOLE REINFORCEMENT STICKERS (3 PER ALIEN)

TOOLS:
- ❤ SCISSORS
- ❤ PENCIL
- ❤ STANDARD ¼ IN PAPER HOLE PUNCH
- ❤ TOOTHPICK
- ❤ TACKY GLUE
- ❤ ULTRA FINE POINT BLACK MARKER
- ❤ SCOTCH TAPE

These inhabitants of a game in the Pizza Planet arcade worship "The Claw," who looms above and periodically drops down to select one of them. Made with extraterrestrial-green craft paper, this alien garland is an out-of-this-world decoration for your child's *Toy Story* party.

INSTRUCTIONS

STEP 1 Using the Three-Eyed Aliens Garland template on page 170, make a photocopy enlarging it 200 percent. Carefully cut out the chain of three aliens—this will be your master template.

STEP 2 Trace the template three times onto a sheet of bright green craft paper. Cut out each three-alien chain and adhere three paper hole reinforcement stickers across the top portion of each alien's face, placing the center sticker ¼ inch from the top of the head and the left and right stickers slightly lower, about $^1/_{16}$ inch apart from the center sticker.

STEP 3 Use the hole punch and a sheet of black craft paper to punch out pupils for the aliens' eyes, making three pupils for each alien. Use a toothpick to apply a tiny dab of tacky glue to the back of each pupil and adhere it in the center of each reinforcement sticker.

STEP 4 Use a pencil to lightly draw a wide smile onto the face of each alien. Go over the pencil with an ultra fine point black marker.

STEP 5 With the black marker, draw vertical lines separating adjacent aliens' ears. Also draw small marks at the top and bottom edges of each ear where it adjoins the alien's head.

STEP 6 To make antennae for the aliens, cut a couple long strips of green craft paper ⅛ inch wide. Cut the strips into 1½-inch portions, creating one antenna for each alien. Apply tacky glue to the bottom ¼ inch of each antenna and adhere it to the center of the back of each alien's head. Use the hole punch to punch circles out of the bright green craft paper, making one circle for each alien. Apply tacky glue to the back of each circle and adhere it at the top of an alien's antenna.

STEP 7 To assemble the garland, place the three-alien chains face down on your work surface. Overlap the rightmost ear of one chain slightly with the leftmost ear of another and adhere with tacky glue. Repeat until all chains have been glued together. Reinforce the bonds by applying strips of Scotch tape on the back of the garland to secure the glue joints.

WOODY'S COWBOY BOOT FAVORS

Woody has been known to utter, "There's a snake in my boot!" when his pull-string is tugged. In this case, Woody's boot contains a much sweeter surprise. To make these spur-rific favors, you'll fashion cowboy boots out of craft paper and fill each one with a handful of candy, toys, or another take-home treat of your choice.

INSTRUCTIONS

STEP 1 Using the Woody's Cowboy Boot Favor template on page 170, make a photocopy enlarging it 200 percent. Carefully cut out all of the shapes—this will be your master template.

STEP 2 For each favor, trace two boot pieces, a vertical strap, a horizontal strap, and two pull straps onto a sheet of reddish-brown heavyweight craft paper. Cut out the pieces.

STEP 3 Trace the sole/heel template piece onto a sheet of dark brown heavyweight craft paper and cut it out.

STEP 4 Trace two spur straps onto a sheet of yellow heavyweight craft paper and cut them out.

STEP 5 Place the dark brown sole/heel piece on your work surface and position one of the reddish-brown boot pieces on top of it so about 1/8 inch of the sole and about ¾ inch of the heel are visible below the lower edge of the boot. Use a pencil to trace a faint line on the sole/heel piece along the edge of the boot piece. Set the boot piece aside and use the stiff paintbrush to apply

MATERIALS

- WOODY'S COWBOY BOOT FAVOR TEMPLATE (P. 170)
- 1 (9 IN BY 12 IN) SHEET OF REDDISH-BROWN HEAVYWEIGHT CRAFT PAPER (WILL MAKE 1 FAVOR)
- 1 (9 IN BY 12 IN) SHEET OF DARK BROWN HEAVYWEIGHT CRAFT PAPER (WILL MAKE 10 FAVORS)
- 1 (9 IN BY 12 IN) SHEET OF YELLOW HEAVYWEIGHT CRAFT PAPER (WILL MAKE AT LEAST 12 FAVORS)
- 2 (½ IN) ROUND DECORATIVE BUTTONS (METALLIC GOLD OR SILVER WORKS BEST)
- 2 (1 IN) ROUND DECORATIVE BUTTONS (METALLIC GOLD OR SILVER WORKS BEST)
- ASSORTED SMALL TRINKETS AND CANDIES

TOOLS:
- SCISSORS
- PENCIL
- TACKY GLUE
- SMALL STIFF PAINTBRUSH

NOTE → The materials can be scaled up for the number of guests invited to your party.

tacky glue to the sole/heel piece in the area above the pencil line. Replace the boot piece, bottom edge flush with the pencil line, and press it gently to adhere. Flip the assembled pieces over.

STEP 6 Set the second boot piece on your work surface next to the flipped-over assembled boot piece so that the toes of the boots are facing each other. Apply a thin bead of glue around the perimeter of the second boot piece and then flip over, positioning atop the assembled boot piece so the top and side edges are flush. Press gently to adhere and then set aside to dry completely.

STEP 7 Fold the vertical strap in half. With the free ends pointing toward the top of the boot, slide the folded strap onto the sole, just forward of the heel. The fold in the strap should rest against the edge of the sole, in the notch right next to the heel. And one free end of the strap should come up over each side of the boot. Use tacky glue to adhere the ends of the strap to the boot.

STEP 8 Fold the horizontal strap in half. With the free ends pointing toward the back of the boot, slide the folded strap onto the front face of the boot, just above the arch of the foot. The tips of the horizontal strap should just overlap the tips of the vertical strap, forming a 90-degree angle. Use tacky glue to adhere the ends of the strap to the boot.

STEP 9 Place the yellow spur straps on your work surface so the round ends are facing each other. Apply glue to the surfaces of the spur straps that are currently face-up. Adhere the spur straps to the boot, one on each of the boot's faces, in line with the horizontal straps, so that the square ends of the spur straps overlap the junction of the vertical and horizontal straps, and the glue-covered round

ends stick to each other behind the back edge of the boot.

STEP 10 Fold both of the pull straps in half, but do not make creases in the paper. Apply glue to the inside ½ inch of each free end. Adhere the first pull strap at the top edge of the boot, in the center, so the glue-covered free ends of the pull strap are gripping the face of the boot and the folded end of the pull strap is oriented up. Flip the boot over and repeat on the other face with the second pull strap.

STEP 11 Apply glue to the backs of the two ½-inch buttons. Adhere one on each face of the boot at the end of the yellow spur strap where it meets the horizontal strap.

STEP 12 Apply glue to the backs of the two 1-inch buttons. Adhere one on each face of the rounded end of the yellow spur strap. Let the glue dry completely before filling the boot with small trinkets and candy.

CHEESY WHEEZYS

MAKES ABOUT 30 STUFFED OLIVES

MATERIALS

- ❤ 1 (6 OZ) CAN EXTRA-LARGE PITTED BLACK OLIVES
- ❤ 1 (4 OZ TO 8 OZ) BALL OF FRESH MOZZARELLA
- ❤ ¼ MEDIUM RED BELL PEPPER

TOOLS:
- ❤ PAPER TOWELS
- ❤ PARING KNIFE
- ❤ 1 (¾ IN BY ½ IN) OVAL FONDANT CUTTER
- ❤ TOOTHPICK (OPTIONAL)

A penguin squeaky toy who makes his debut in *Toy Story 2*, Wheezy gets his name from his broken squeaker. After narrowly escaping Andy's family yard sale, Wheezy is supplied with a new squeaker—courtesy of Mr. Shark—and surprises everyone with his crooning abilities! Black, white, and dressed in a dapper red bow tie, these olive-and-mozzarella snacks are just as irresistible as Wheezy himself.

INSTRUCTIONS

STEP 1   Drain the olives and blot with paper towels to dry completely. Use a small paring knife to slice off one face of each olive. Be careful not to remove too much; the goal is to leave most of the olive intact.

STEP 2   Cut the mozzarella piece into ½-inch slices. Use the fondant cutter to cut out a tuxedo shirt for each olive. Gently press a mozzarella oval into each olive, taking care not to press too hard, as this can cause the olive to split. (Tip: you can use the paring knife to carve away some of the inside of the olive to make room for the mozzarella oval, if necessary. A toothpick also works well as a tool to tuck the edges of the cheese inside the olive.)

STEP 3   To create bow ties, use the paring knife to cut very tiny triangular slivers out of the red bell pepper. Arrange two triangles in a bow tie shape atop the mozzarella oval, about ⅛ to ¼ inch from one narrow end. Refrigerate until ready to serve.

WOODY'S SHERIFF BADGE SANDWICHES

MAKES 8 OPEN-FACE SANDWICHES

MATERIALS

- 12 SLICES PROVOLONE CHEESE OR FAVORITE SLICED CHEESE, AT LEAST ⅛ IN THICK
- 8 SLICES OF BREAD
- 1 TO 2 TBSP SOFTENED BUTTER

TOOLS:

- WAX PAPER
- 1 (3¼ IN) STAR-SHAPED COOKIE OR FONDANT CUTTER
- 1 (2½ IN) STAR-SHAPED COOKIE OR FONDANT CUTTER
- 1 (⅜ IN) METAL PASTRY BAG TIP OR CIRCULAR FONDANT CUTTER
- FLAT TRAY
- PLASTIC WRAP
- SMALL SPATULA (OPTIONAL)

There are a few important things a cowboy needs in order to be a sheriff in the wild West: a trusty horse (in Woody's case, Bullseye), a pair of boots with spurs, and a shiny sheriff's badge. This sandwich platter evokes Woody's gold-star insignia and can be made with many varieties of bread and cheese.

INSTRUCTIONS

STEP 1 Cover the work surface with a sheet of wax paper. Use the larger star-shaped cookie or fondant cutter to cut eight star-shaped pieces from the cheese slices. Use the smaller star-shaped cookie or fondant cutter to cut an additional eight star-shaped pieces from the cheese slices. Each slice of cheese should yield one large star and two smaller stars.

STEP 2 Use the metal pastry bag tip or circular fondant cutter to cut forty circles from the remaining cheese slices.

STEP 3   Center one of the smaller cheese stars on top of each of the larger cheese stars. Then gently press a cheese circle onto each of the five points of each star.

STEP 4   Transfer the sheet of wax paper topped with the assembled cheese stars onto a flat tray. Cover with a piece of plastic wrap and refrigerate while you prepare the bread.

STEP 5   Use the larger star-shaped cutter to cut one star from each slice of bread or tortilla. (Tip: you can use the scraps to make fresh croutons or breadcrumbs for a different recipe.) Spread a little butter on each of the bread stars.

STEP 6   Remove the cheese stars from the refrigerator and place one on top of each buttered bread star. A small spatula comes in handy for this. Place sandwiches back on tray and cover with plastic wrap. Refrigerate until ready to serve.

BUZZ LIGHTYEAR CAKE

MAKES 1 (2 LAYER) 8 IN OR 9 IN ROUND CAKE

MATERIALS

- BUZZ LIGHTYEAR CAKE TEMPLATE (P. 170)

INGREDIENTS:

- 1 (24 OZ) PACKAGE WHITE, READY-TO-USE FONDANT
- PINK FOOD COLORING
- PURPLE FOOD COLORING
- GREEN FOOD COLORING
- BROWN FOOD COLORING
- BLUE FOOD COLORING
- BLACK FOOD COLORING
- POWDERED SUGAR, FOR ROLLING
- 2 WHITE SUGAR PEARLS
- FAVORITE RECIPE FOR A 2-LAYER 8- OR 9-INCH ROUND CAKE, PREPARED AND FROSTED

TOOLS:

- SCISSORS
- PLASTIC WRAP
- KITCHEN GLOVES (OPTIONAL)
- WAX PAPER
- ROLLING PIN
- SHARP KITCHEN KNIFE
- PUSHPIN
- 1 (1 IN) CIRCULAR FONDANT CUTTER (OPTIONAL)
- TOOTHPICK
- 1 (5/8 IN) CIRCULAR FONDANT CUTTER (OPTIONAL)
- 1 (3/8 IN) CIRCULAR FONDANT CUTTER (OPTIONAL)

When Buzz Lightyear first finds himself in Andy's room, he firmly believes that he is *the* Buzz Lightyear—stranded on a foreign planet, able to fly, and armed with a stunning laser beam. This round cake is the perfect dessert to make for a *Toy Story* party; topped with a fondant depiction of the space ranger's face, it is sure to stun your child's guests with amazement. To infinity ... and beyond!

INSTRUCTIONS

STEP 1 Using the Buzz Lightyear Cake template on page 170, make a photocopy enlarging it 200 percent. Carefully cut out all of the shapes— this is your master template.

STEP 2 Divide the fondant into four equal parts (about 6 ounces each). Add pink food coloring to one quarter and knead (wearing kitchen gloves is a good idea) until the color is uniform and a shade resembling Buzz's skin tone is achieved. Wrap tightly in plastic wrap and set aside.

STEP 3   Add purple food coloring to the second quarter of fondant and knead until the color is uniform and the desired shade is achieved. Wrap tightly in plastic wrap and set aside.

STEP 4   Add green food coloring to the third quarter of fondant and knead until the color is uniform and the desired shade is achieved. Wrap tightly in plastic wrap and set aside.

STEP 5   Of the remaining quarter of white fondant, reserve half of it, wrap tightly in plastic wrap, and set it aside. Divide the rest into three equal portions. Add brown food coloring to one portion, blue food coloring to the second portion, and black food coloring to the third portion. Knead each until colors are uniform, wrap in plastic wrap, and set aside.

STEP 6   Cover work surface with a sheet of wax paper and sprinkle with powdered sugar. Unwrap pink fondant and roll out to a ⅜-inch thickness, dusting the fondant and rolling pin with additional powdered sugar if it begins to stick. Place the face template piece on top of the rolled-out fondant and use a sharp kitchen knife to trace around the outside edge. Remove excess. Transfer the fondant and template to a new sheet of wax paper dusted with powdered sugar.

STEP 7   To create guiding marks for the fondant facial features that will be added later, use a pushpin to poke through the paper and fondant at the centers of the eye circles and at several points along the nose, smile, and chin dimple lines.

STEP 8   Remove the paper face template piece (reserving for later use) and place the teeth template piece in its proper position based on the holes poked around Buzz's smile in step 7. Cut around the edge of the teeth template piece with a sharp kitchen knife and remove the resulting piece of pink fondant.

STEP 9   Cut the circular holes where Buzz's eyes will go. You can use the eye template piece (as the teeth piece was used in step 8) or you can use a 1-inch circular fondant cutter. Remove the resulting pieces of pink fondant.

STEP 10   Use the tip of the knife to cut along the nose, smile, and chin dimple lines, etching them into the pink fondant face. Then use the tip of a toothpick to gently press down into the lines, smoothing and widening them slightly. Cover the face with plastic wrap and set aside.

STEP 11   Cover the work surface with a new sheet of wax paper and sprinkle with powdered sugar. Unwrap purple fondant and roll out to a ⅜-inch thickness, dusting the fondant and rolling pin with additional powdered sugar if it begins to stick. Place the hood template piece on top of the rolled-out fondant and use a sharp kitchen knife to trace around it. Reserve hood template piece for later use. Then use the ear coverings template piece to cut out a pair of purple ovals.

STEP 12   Uncover the pink fondant face piece and position the purple hood piece around it. Set one of the purple ear covering pieces in place on top of the left side of the hood, using a drop of water to adhere it. Tuck the edge of the remaining purple ear covering piece underneath the right edge of the face, just beside the eye opening. Use a drop of water to adhere it. Cover the face with plastic wrap again and set aside.

STEP 13 Cover the work surface with a new sheet of wax paper and sprinkle with powdered sugar. Unwrap white fondant and roll out to a ⅜-inch thickness, dusting the fondant and rolling pin with additional powdered sugar if it begins to stick. Place the teeth template piece on top of the rolled-out fondant and use a sharp kitchen knife to trace around it. Then use the eye white template piece (or the 1-inch circular fondant cutter) to cut out a pair of circles.

STEP 14 Use the knife to cut along the line between the top and bottom teeth, as indicated in the template. Uncover the pink fondant face and insert the white teeth piece into the hole you cut in step 8. Insert the eye white pieces into the holes cut in step 9. Cover the face with plastic wrap again and set aside.

STEP 15 Cover the work surface with a new sheet of wax paper and sprinkle with powdered sugar. Unwrap blue fondant and roll out to a ⅜-inch thickness, dusting the fondant and rolling pin with additional powdered sugar if it begins to stick. Place the iris template piece on top of the rolled-out fondant and use a sharp kitchen knife to trace around it twice. Alternately, you can use the ⅝-inch circular fondant cutter to make two blue irises.

STEP 16 Uncover the pink fondant face. Use either

the paper iris template piece or the ⅝-inch circular fondant cutter to cut a hole in the center of each eye white. Remove the resulting circles of white fondant and insert the blue irises. Cover the face with plastic wrap again and set aside.

STEP 17 Cover the work surface with a new sheet of wax paper and sprinkle with powdered sugar. Unwrap black fondant and roll out to a ⅜-inch thickness, dusting the fondant and rolling pin with additional powdered sugar if it begins to stick. Place the pupil template piece on top of the rolled-out fondant and use a sharp kitchen knife to trace around it twice. Alternately, you can use the ⅜-inch circular fondant cutter to make two black pupils.

STEP 18 Uncover the pink fondant face. Use either the paper pupil template piece or a ⅜-inch circular fondant cutter to cut a hole in the center of each blue iris. Remove the resulting circles of blue fondant and insert the black pupils.

STEP 19 To complete the eyes, place a white sugar pearl on the leftmost edge of each pupil. Use the tip of a toothpick to push the sugar pearls down into the fondant slightly. Cover the face with plastic wrap again and set aside.

STEP 20 Cover the work surface with

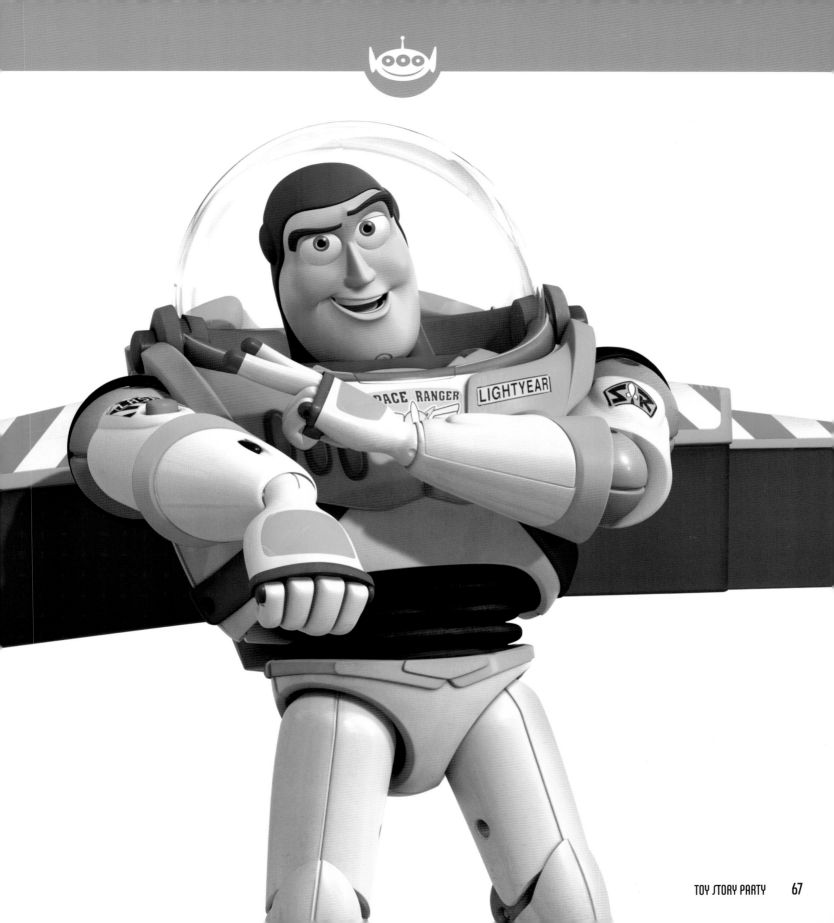

a new sheet of wax paper and sprinkle with powdered sugar. Unwrap brown fondant and roll out to a ⅜-inch thickness, dusting the fondant and rolling pin with additional powdered sugar if it begins to stick. Place the left eyebrow template piece and the right eyebrow template piece on top of the rolled-out fondant and use a sharp kitchen knife to trace around them.

STEP 21 Uncover the pink fondant face. Place the left eyebrow just above the left eye, using a drop of water to adhere it to the face. Place the right eyebrow slightly higher so the curve is flush with the upper right edge of Buzz's face, and use a drop of water to adhere it. Cover the face with plastic wrap again and set aside.

STEP 22 Cover the work surface with a new sheet of wax paper and sprinkle with powdered sugar. Unwrap green fondant and roll out to a ⅜-inch thickness, dusting the fondant and rolling pin with additional powdered sugar if it begins to stick. Place the background template piece on top of the rolled-out fondant and use a sharp kitchen knife to trace around it.

STEP 23 Position the paper face template piece and the hood template piece together atop the green fondant semicircle so that the flat top of the semicircle is level with the bottom edge of Buzz's teeth. Trace around the template pieces with the tip of a knife, removing the resulting piece of green fondant. Cover assembled piece in plastic wrap until ready to use. (Tip: if wrapped tightly, fondant pieces can be made several days in advance of the party.)

STEP 24 Prepare your favorite recipe for a 2-layer 8- or 9-inch cake. Once frosted in desired icing (an even layer of white buttercream works well), top the cake with the assembled Buzz head and the green fondant background piece. (Tip: if you prefer, you can roll out an additional portion of white fondant, cut an 8- or 9-inch circle to fit the top of the cake, and place it atop the frosting first to serve as a base layer for Buzz's face.)

WOODY'S WINK

GAME FOR 10–25 GUESTS

MATERIALS

- A DECK OF CARDS
- A LIVING ROOM
- GUESTS

Sherrif Woody knows a lot of different ways to disable his opponent. One of them is to give his adversary the Wink of Woody.

INSTRUCTIONS

STEP 1 Gather the guests in a tight circle. The more the better, as it is easier to hide in great numbers.

STEP 2 Distribute as many cards from the deck as are in the group. Be sure to include the Ace of Spades as it is this card which decides who will be Woody. Everyone places their card face down on the flor or table in front of them and waits for the first wink.

STEP 3 The guests in the circle are Woody's opponents. It is Woody's mission to secretly wink his adversaries out of ther game. He has to be very careful and no one may see him wink.

STEP 4 When someone gets winked by Woody they have to flip over their card and place it in the middle of the group and declare their expulsion.

STEP 5 If Woody gets caught winking he is challenged and has to flip over his card and the game is over. If the challenge is wrong then the accuser is out.

MICKEY & MINNIE
PARTY

Mickey and Minnie Mouse first appeared together in the shorts *Plane Crazy, The Gallopin' Gaucho,* and *Steamboat Willie* between 1928 and 1929. Since then, they have been one of Hollywood's most enduring couples, headlining numerous short films, television shows, movies, theme park attractions, books, magazines, comics, and video games. With their plucky personalities and everyman characteristics, Mickey and Minnie remain favorites across generations of fans.

While their animation has evolved over the decades, certain things about Mickey and Minnie have remained constant since the 1940s: white gloves, yellow shoes, red shorts, a polka-dot dress, and matching hair bow are signature parts of the characters' designs. Not to mention their mouse ears! Those iconic elements take center stage in this birthday party, which includes Mickey Mouse Glove Invitations, a Hidden Mickey Scavenger Hunt, and Mickey and Minnie Mouse Ears. Kids will love nibbling at Minnie's Pizza Polka Dots, Mickey's Chips and Dips, and Mickey Mouse Sandwich Cookies. And each guest can take home a Mickey Mouse Candy Cup as a party favor!

MICKEY MOUSE GLOVE INVITATION

MAKES 2 INVITATIONS

MATERIALS

- ❦ MICKEY MOUSE GLOVE INVITATION TEMPLATE (P. 167)
- ❦ 1 (12 IN BY 12 IN) SHEET WHITE CARD STOCK
- ❦ ENVELOPES (OPTIONAL)

TOOLS:
- ❦ PENCIL (DULL)
- ❦ SCISSORS
- ❦ RULER
- ❦ PAPER CUTTER (OPTIONAL)
- ❦ EMBOSSING STYLUS (OPTIONAL)
- ❦ FINE POINT BLACK MARKER

NOTE → The materials can be scaled up for the number of guests invited to your party.

Mickey's signature white gloves have been around since 1935. To get your Mickey and Minnie party off on the right foot (or hand!), send these glove-shaped invitations to your child's friends.

INSTRUCTIONS

STEP 1 Using the Mickey Mouse Glove Invitation template on page 167, make a photocopy enlarging it 200 percent. Carefully cut out the glove—this will be your master template.

STEP 2 Using a pencil, ruler, and scissors—or a paper cutter if preferred—measure and cut out a 10-by-5-inch rectangle of white card stock. Fold in half, bringing the two shorter ends together. Place the template cutout on top of the folded card stock with the thumb extending just a bit (about ⅛ inch) past the fold. Trace around the edge of the template.

STEP 3 To transfer the pleat markings to the invite, use a dull pencil point or embossing stylus to trace the ovals, making a slight indent in the card stock underneath.

STEP 4 Cut along the traced outline of the glove, going through both layers of the folded card stock, and leaving the fold at the end of the thumb intact.

STEP 5 Use a fine point black marker to fill in the ovals on the outside of the glove. Then add the party information—place, date, location, RSVP instructions—on the inside of the glove. Place in envelopes, if using.

NOTE These invitations fit in a standard 4½-by-5-inch rectangular or 5-inch square envelope.

HIDDEN MICKEY SCAVENGER HUNT

MAKES MANY HIDDEN MICKEYS

MATERIALS

- ❤ CARD STOCK IN ASSORTED COLORS
- ❤ CRAFT PAPER IN ASSORTED COLORS (SOLID AND/OR PATTERNS)

TOOLS:

- ❤ 1 (2 IN) CIRCULAR PAPER CUTTER
- ❤ 1 (1 IN) CIRCULAR PAPER CUTTER
- ❤ 1 (⅝ IN) CIRCULAR PAPER CUTTER
- ❤ GLUE STICK

NOTE The materials can be scaled up for the number of guests invited to your party. Plan for three to five Hidden Mickeys per guest.

What are comprised of three circles—one large and two small—and represent one of the most popular animated characters in the world? What appears all over Walt Disney World and Disneyland Resort in plain sight, yet are often difficult to find? Hidden Mickeys! Use this pattern for making your own Hidden Mickeys and create a scavenger hunt in your home.

INSTRUCTIONS

STEP 1 Determine the total number of Hidden Mickeys to be created based on the area of the house that will be used for the scavenger hunt, the number of guests, and the degree of difficulty desired. Use the 2-inch circular paper puncher to cut the corresponding number of circles out of card stock in a variety of colors.

STEP 2 Use the 1-inch and ⅝-inch circular paper punchers to cut sets of circles (one 1-inch Mickey head and two ⅝-inch Mickey ears) out of assorted colors of craft paper.

STEP 3 For each Hidden Mickey, choose a card stock circle in a color that contrasts well with each set of head-and-ears circles. Use the glue stick to glue down the ears, positioning them ¼ inch apart from each other. Then glue down the head, overlapping the bottoms of the ears just slightly. Allow to dry completely.

Before the party begins, the Mickeys should be hidden in an area of the house that will not be populated during the majority of the celebration. The Mickeys should be hidden in plain sight, but only visible from certain angles—for example, against the inside wall of a bookcase on a shelf at knee level. The child who collects the most Hidden Mickeys in the time given wins a prize.

MICKEY AND MINNIE MOUSE EARS

MAKES 1 SET OF EARS

MATERIALS

- MICKEY AND MINNIE MOUSE EARS TEMPLATE (P. 167)
- 2 (8 ½ IN BY 4 ½ IN) RECTANGLES STIFF BLACK FELT
- 1 BLACK HEADBAND
- 1 (20 IN) LENGTH OF RED-AND-WHITE POLKA-DOTTED RIBBON, 2 IN WIDE (FOR MINNIE)
- 1 (3 IN) LENGTH OF RED-AND-WHITE POLKA-DOTTED RIBBON, 2 IN WIDE (FOR MINNIE)

TOOLS:

- SCISSORS
- STRAIGHT PINS
- LOW-TEMPERATURE HOT GLUE GUN

NOTE → The materials can be scaled up for the number of guests invited to your party.

Mickey Mouse ears have long been a treasured souvenir from Disney theme parks. They come in varieties ranging from blue topped with a sorcerer's hat to pink topped with a tiara. This pattern for homemade Mickey and Minnie ears is a fantastic way to induct your little Mouseketeers into the Mickey Mouse Club and make a great favor.

INSTRUCTIONS

STEP 1 Using the Mickey and Minnie Mouse Ears template on page 167, make a photocopy enlarging it 200 percent. Carefully cut out the shapes—this will be your master template.

STEP 2 Place the template on a rectangle of stiff black felt. Use straight pins to pin the template to the felt and then cut around it. Repeat with another rectangle of black felt to create a second ear.

STEP 3 Working with one ear piece at a time, apply hot glue along the center line of the felt (as specified on the template). Adhere the glued portion to the underside of the headband about 1¼ inches left of the center point of the headband. Now fold the two round ear portions up over the band and apply additional hot glue to glue them together. Repeat with the second ear piece, gluing it 1¼ inches to the right of center so that the ears are spaced about 2½ inches apart.

JTEP 4 For a Minnie headband, create a bow by folding the 20-inch length of polka-dot ribbon in thirds. One loose end should be on the bottom, and the other loose end should be inside one of the folds. Apply a small amount of hot glue to one end of the 3-inch length of ribbon and adhere it to the midpoint of the underside of the folded longer ribbon. Wrap the short piece all the way around the midpoint of the folded longer ribbon, cinching it just a bit, and secure the end by gluing the ribbon to itself on the underside. Apply additional hot glue to the underside of the bow's midpoint and adhere to the headband between the two ears.

MICKEY MOUSE CANDY CUPS

MAKES 1 FAVOR

MATERIALS

- ❤ 1 (8½ IN BY 11 IN) SHEET BLACK CARD STOCK
- ❤ 1 (8½ IN BY 11 IN) SHEET RED CARD STOCK
- ❤ 2 SMALL WHITE BUTTONS
- ❤ PLASTIC WRAP OR CLEAR CELLOPHANE
- ❤ BLACK JELLY BEANS (OR OTHER CANDY OF YOUR CHOOSING)
- ❤ NARROW RED RIBBON OR RED TWIST TIES

TOOLS:

- ❤ RULER
- ❤ PENCIL
- ❤ SCISSORS
- ❤ GLUE STICK
- ❤ CARDBOARD PAPER TOWEL TUBE (OPTIONAL)
- ❤ TACKY GLUE

> **NOTE** The materials can be scaled up for the number of guests invited to your party.

From the roaring twenties to the flower-power sixties, through the disco fever seventies to the skinny-jeans modern era, Mickey's choice in duds has not changed; he is forever adorned in bright red shorts with two big white buttons. Simply evoking the mouse's classic style, these party favors are made with black and red card stock and white buttons, and then filled with the treat of your choice!

INSTRUCTIONS

STEP 1   Use a ruler, pencil, and a pair of scissors to measure and cut a 2¼-by-8½-inch rectangle of black card stock and a 1½-by-8½-inch rectangle of red card stock.

STEP 2   Apply the glue stick to the back of the red rectangle, and then adhere atop the black rectangle, lining up the long lower edges.

STEP 3   Roll the double-layered rectangle into a cylinder about two inches in diameter, overlapping the ends quite a bit and gluing them together. (Tip: roll the card stock around a cardboard paper towel tube and then slip the tube out once you've glued the ends.)

STEP 4   Apply a small dab of tacky glue to the back of two small white buttons and adhere to the front of the tube, about ¼ inch from the top edge of the red card stock and about ⅜ inch apart from each other.

STEP 5   While the glue is drying, cut a piece of plastic wrap or clear cellophane approximately 8 inches square. Place a small handful of black jelly beans (or other candies)

in the center and gather up the edges of the plastic wrap around the treat. Tie off with a 5-inch length of narrow red ribbon or a red twist tie.

STEP 6 Once the glue on the candy cup has dried, place the treat baggy inside. Give one to each guest as a party favor.

MICKEY'S CHIPS AND DIPS

MATERIALS

- ❦ LARGE RED BELL PEPPER (WIDE AND SYMMETRICAL)
- ❦ THICK (½ INCH OR SO) SLICE OF FRESH MOZZARELLA CHEESE
- ❦ HUMMUS, BLACK BEAN, OR OTHER FAVORITE DIP
- ❦ BLUE CORN CHIPS

TOOLS:

- ❦ KITCHEN OR CHEF'S KNIFE
- ❦ 1 (½ IN BY ¾ IN) OVAL FONDANT CUTTER

Mickey's signature shorts are adapted to a tasty snack with Mickey's Chips and Dips. Made with hollowed-out red bell peppers, these dip bowls can be filled with hummus, black bean dip, or your favorite spread and served with blue corn chips that echo Mickey's ears.

INSTRUCTIONS

STEP 1 Wash the pepper and slice the top off as close to the stem as possible. Carefully remove the inner veins and seeds. If the pepper won't stand upright on its own, cut a thin slice off the bottom to level it.

STEP 2 Use the fondant cutter to cut two small oval holes in the face of the pepper from the inside out. Position the holes about ¾ inch apart with the tops about ¾ inch down from the pepper's upper edge.

STEP 3 Cut two matching ovals from the slice of mozzarella, and use them to fill the holes in the pepper. Then fill the pepper with hummus or dip, and serve with plenty of corn chips.

MINNIE'S MOZZARELLA POLKA DOTS

MAKES ABOUT 36 MINI PIZZAS

MATERIALS

- OLIVE OIL, FOR GREASING
- 1 LB PIZZA DOUGH
- FLOUR, FOR ROLLING
- 1 (1 LB) BALL/CHUNK MOZZARELLA CHEESE
- 1 (14 OZ) JAR PIZZA SAUCE

TOOLS:

- TWO LARGE BAKING SHEETS
- ROLLING PIN
- 1 (2¼ IN) CIRCULAR COOKIE OR BISCUIT CUTTER
- 1 (1 IN) CIRCULAR COOKIE OR FONDANT CUTTER

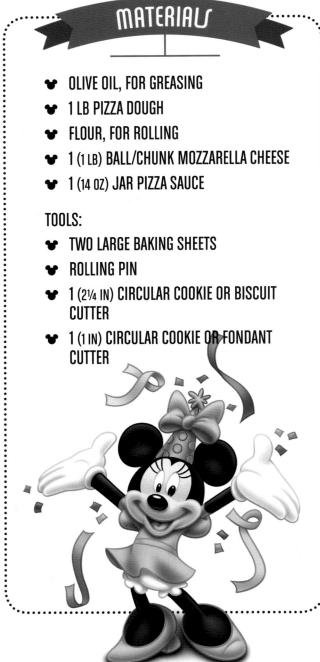

Like Mickey, Minnie has had starring roles that required her to assume different personas—and outfits. She has played a princess, a hula girl, and a nurse, just to name a few! But she always comes back to her favorite fashionable pattern: polka dots. With contrasting red tomato sauce and white mozzarella "dots," these mini pizzas are definitely in vogue!

INSTRUCTIONS

STEP 1 Preheat oven to 400°F. Use olive oil to lightly grease baking sheets.

STEP 2 On a lightly floured surface, roll out the dough to ¼-inch thickness. Use the 2¼-inch circular cookie or biscuit cutter to cut out as many circles as possible, approximately three dozen. Place on prepared baking sheets, leaving at least ½ inch between dough circles, and set aside.

STEP 3 Slice the mozzarella into ⅜-inch-thick slices. Use the 1-inch circular cookie or fondant cutter to cut out as many circles of cheese as there are dough circles. Chill in refrigerator until ready to use.

STEP 4 Top each dough circle with a spoonful of pizza sauce. Place in oven and bake until the bottoms are lightly browned, about 5 minutes.

STEP 5   Remove the baking sheets from oven and top each dough circle with a mozzarella polka dot. Return baking sheets to the oven and bake just long enough so that cheese begins to melt but does not lose its shape, about 2 minutes.

STEP 6   Repeat steps 4 and 5 with remaining batches of dough circles. Cool slightly before serving.

NOTE

If you don't have cutters in the specified sizes, you can improvise. For example, you can use the base of a metal pastry bag tip or a bottle cap. Alternatively, you can use 1½- and 2¾-inch cutters, or pair other circles with comparable size ratios.

MICKEY MOUSE SANDWICH COOKIES

MAKES 12 COOKIES

MATERIALS

- 1 LB CHOCOLATE SUGAR COOKIE DOUGH, PREPARED ACCORDING TO FAVORITE RECIPE, CHILLED*
- FLOUR, FOR ROLLING
- 1 (7 OZ) POUCH PREMADE WHITE COOKIE ICING

TOOLS:

- 2 LARGE BAKING SHEETS
- ROLLING PIN
- 1 (3 IN WIDE) MICKEY-SHAPED COOKIE CUTTER
- WIRE RACKS

NOTE

* If your favorite sugar cookie dough recipe tends to spread a lot when baking, try kneading a little more flour into it and then baking a test cookie to make sure it holds its shape.

Every party needs a sweet surpirse. These adorable mouse ear sandwich cookies fit the bill perfectly—especially for a child who likes cookies better than cake. Mickey-shaped cookie cutters can be found in the baking section of a well-stocked craft store and are readily available online.

INSTRUCTIONS

STEP 1 Preheat the oven and prepare baking sheets as specified by your recipe.

STEP 2 On a lightly floured surface, roll out the dough to a ⅜-inch thickness. Using a Mickey-shaped cookie cutter (about 3 inches wide from ear to ear), cut out twenty-four cookies. Place them on prepared baking sheets, spaced per your recipe's instructions, and bake for the amount of time specified in your recipe. Check them a bit early; cookies should be firm but not crisp.

STEP 3 Allow cookies to cool slightly on baking sheets, and then transfer to wire racks to cool completely.

STEP 4 Working with two cookies at a time, turn one over so the flat side is facing up. Pipe a layer of icing onto it, stopping just shy of the edges of the cookie. Place the second cookie, flat side down, on top of the icing and press evenly, just enough so that the icing peeks out of the sides.

STEP 5 Set aside the assembled cookies until the icing has set and then serve.

MICKEY & MINNIE'S OUTDOOR GAMES

GAME FOR 10–25 GUESTS

MATERIALS

- 2 BIG SACKS
- 2 EGGS (HARD BOILED)
- 2 LARGE SPOONS
- 2 COOKIES
- 2 APPLES

Gather everyone arround! It's time for the Official Mickey & Minnie's Outdoor Games! 4 different and exciting tournaments for everyone. Split the guests into two competing teams and let the games begin!

GAME 2: THE EGG RACE

With a spoon in their mouth and an egg on the spoon, one member from each team has to race from one end of the field to the other and back again. Then another member takes over etc. If the egg drops, the member has to begin again from the starting point. First team to finish wins.

GAME 3: THE APPLE RACE

With an apple fixed between their chin and chest, one member from each team has to race from one end of the field to the other and back again. Then another member takes over etc. First team to finish wins.

GAME 4: THE COOKIE TEST

Each team picks out an even number of members (3-5) who then place a cookie on top of their foreheads. Once everyone is ready they will then let the cookie slide down their face and into their mouth. If the cookie falls down they have to begin again. First team to finish wins.

GAME 1: THE SACK JUMP

One member from each team has to jump in a sack from one end of the field to the other and back again. Then another member takes over etc. First team to finish wins.

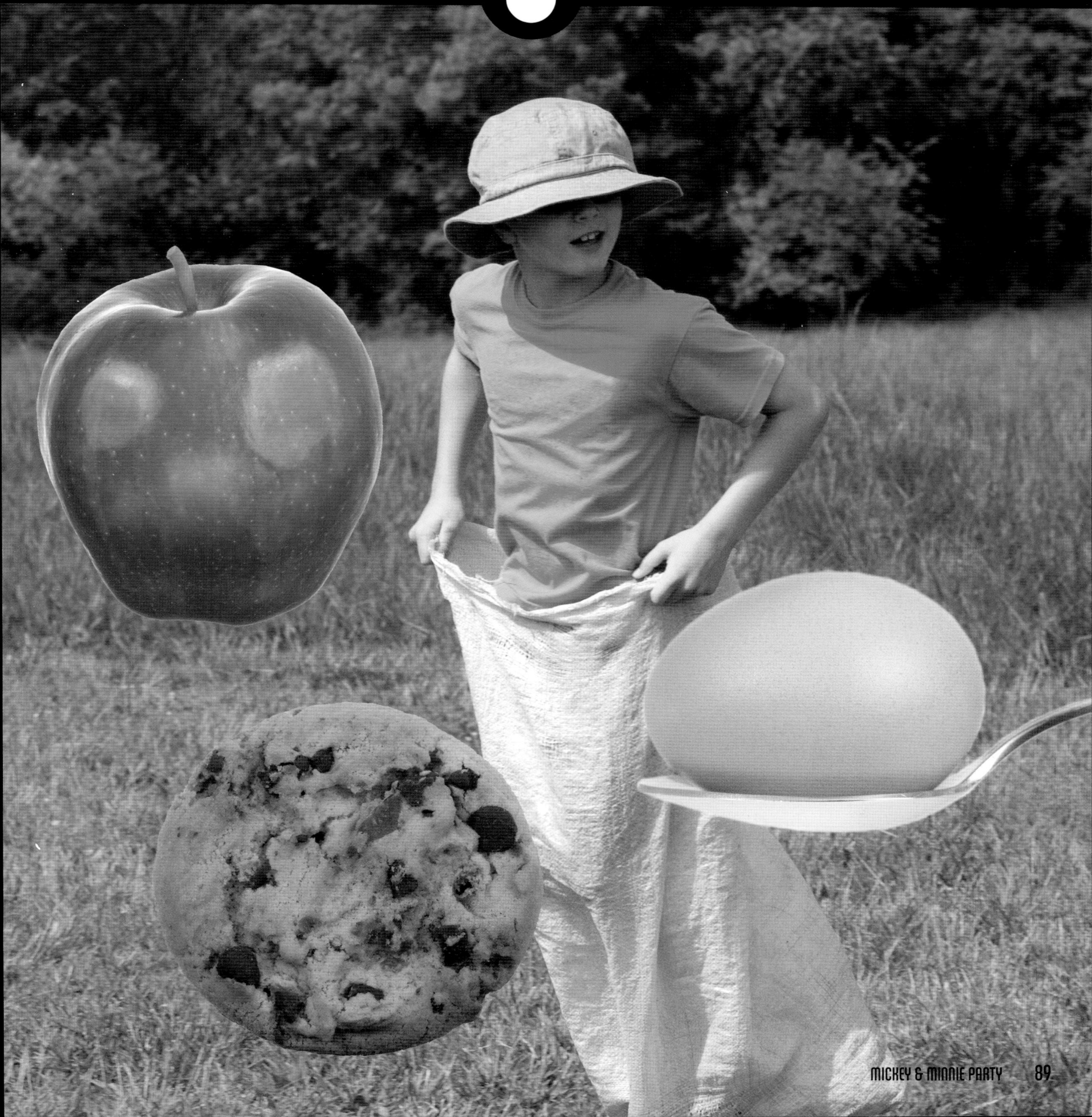

MICKEY'S & MINNIE'S VOICES

GAME FOR 10–25 GUESTS

MATERIALS

- ❤ PAPER
- ❤ PEN

Everyone knows the popular game of trying to guess when someone's acting out a word from a card, right?
Well, here is that game with a twist: All contestants must speak with the high pitched voices of Mickey and Minnie!

INSTRUCTIONS

STEP 1   Split the guests into two even groups.

STEP 2   Each group picks an actor.

STEP 3   The actor is given a bunch of cards with words on them. These words must belong to a certain category. For instance a "food" category would have words like: eggs, ham, chicken etc. It is announced beforehand what the category is.

STEP 4   The actor takes one card and starts to act out the word on it. The group must guess what the actor is trying to explain and recieves one point for each right guess. The actor must be totally silent otherwise the whole group loses a point.

STEP 5   Here is the catch: All the contestants must speak with the high pitched voices of Mickey and Minnie! If they guess right with a normal voice the group loses a point. The group with the most points wins.

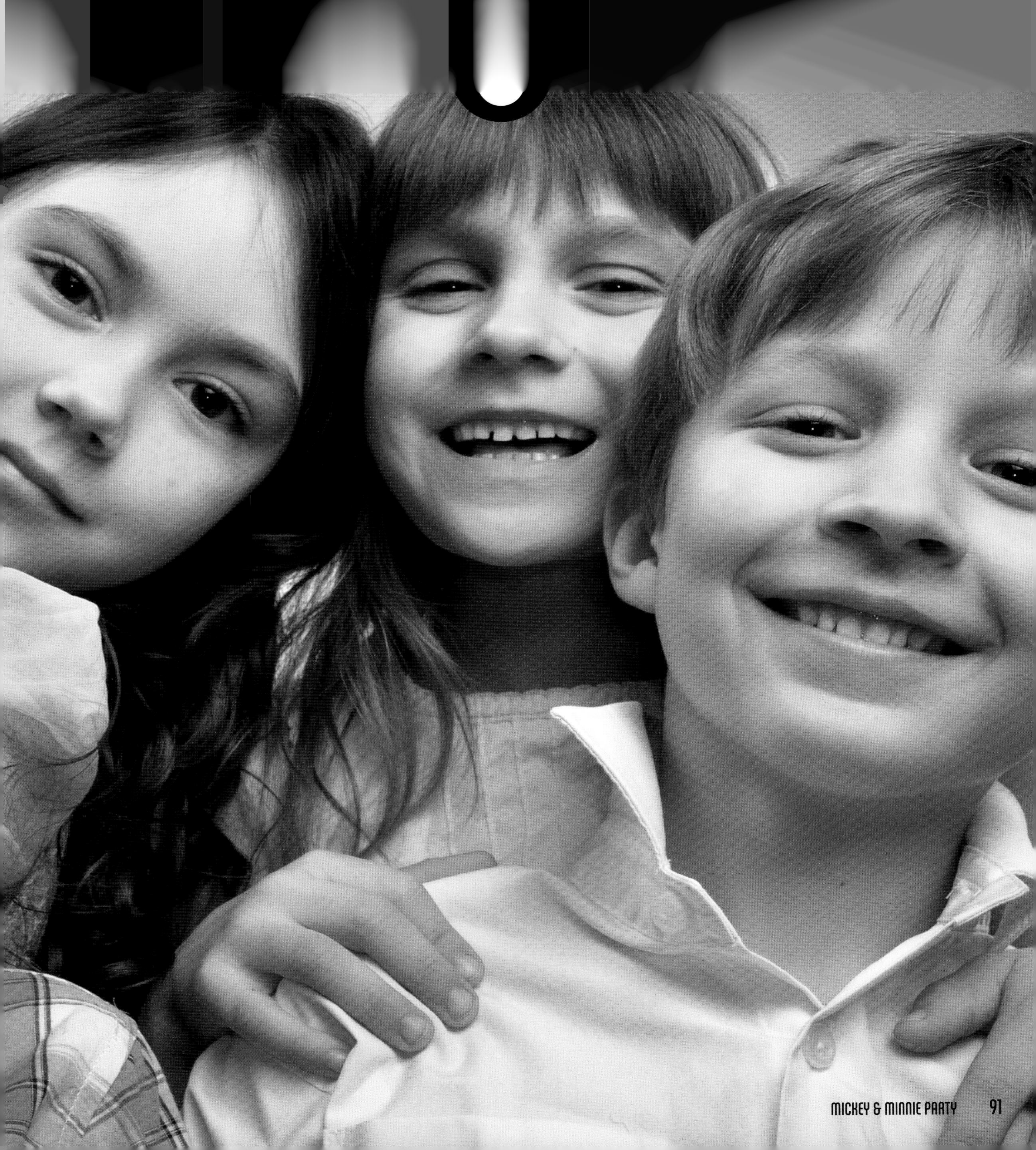

MONSTERS INC. PARTY

Monsters, Inc. (2001) centers on two best friends, Mike Wazowski and James P. Sullivan ("Sulley"), monsters who live in Monstropolis and work at a power company called Monsters, Inc. The power for the city is generated through screams produced by human children when scared by the employees of Monsters, Inc. In the 2013 prequel, *Monsters University*, audiences learn how Mike and Sulley met for the first time—and studied up on all their scare tactics—back in their college days.

In order to throw a *Monsters*-themed party, get things off on the right foot (or tentacle) with Scare Floor Door Invitations. The monstrous fun continues with Sulley Drink Coasters and Mike Wazowski Spoon Puppets, which later become favors. Then serve up some scream-worthy dishes, including Randall Boggs Blueberry Smoothies, Terry and Terri Terrifying Flatbread Sandwiches, and Mike Wazowski Cupcakes. And don't forget to send each child off with a Sulley's Dorm Party Popcorn favor!

SCARE FLOOR DOOR INVITATIONS AND GARLANDS

MATERIALS

- SCARE FLOOR DOOR INVITE/GARLAND TEMPLATE (P. 168)
- 8 (8½ X 11 IN) SHEETS CRAFT PAPER, ALL DIFFERENT LIGHT COLORS
- 8 (8½ X 11 IN) SHEETS CRAFT PAPER, DARKER SHADES OF THE LIGHT COLORS
- 8 SMALL BUTTONS IN A VARIETY OF COLORS (ABOUT ⅜ INCH IN DIAMETER)
- 48-INCH LENGTH THIN RIBBON IN ANY COLOR (FOR THE GARLAND)
- SMALL FLOWER STICKERS (OPTIONAL)

TOOLS:
- SCISSORS
- PENCIL
- GLUE STICK
- TACKY GLUE
- TOOTHPICK
- PACKING TAPE (FOR THE GARLAND)

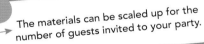

NOTE The materials can be scaled up for the number of guests invited to your party.

Housed in the vast facility of Monsters, Inc. is a massive collection of closet doors, each of which is a portal into a child's bedroom. Armed with a variety of scare tactics, monsters enter the human world through these doors, eliciting the most potent screams possible. These craft paper scare doors are the perfect way to start a *Monsters*-themed party as both invitations and garlands.

INSTRUCTIONS

STEP 1 Using the Scare Floor Door Invite/Garland template on page 168, make a photocopy enlarging it 200 percent. Carefully cut out all of the shapes—this will be your master template. Note: for ease of cutting the nested panel shapes, it may be easier to make two photocopies or tracings and cut the larger panel of each nested pair from one photocopy/tracing, and then cut the smaller panel of each pair from the second photocopy/tracing.

STEP 2 There are five types of door in the template: single panel, double panel, triple panel, eight panel, and Boo's door. For a single-panel door, trace and cut a base door shape from a light shade of any color craft paper. Then trace and cut the smaller of the two interior panels from the same color. Trace and cut the larger of the two interior panels from a shade of craft paper that is darker than the base door, but the same tone. For example, you could use lavender for the base door and smaller panel and grape purple for the larger panel.

STEP 3 To create a double-panel door, trace and cut a base door shape from a light shade of any color craft paper. Then trace and cut two of the smaller of the two interior panels from the same color. Next, trace and cut two of the larger of the two interior panels from a shade of craft paper that is darker than the base door, but the same tone.

STEP 4 To create a triple-panel door, trace and cut a base door shape from a light shade of any color craft paper. Then trace and cut three of the smaller of the two interior panels from the same color. Next, trace and cut three of the larger of the two interior panels from a shade of craft paper that is darker than the base door, but the same tone.

STEP 5 To create an eight-panel door, trace and cut a base door shape from a light shade of any color craft paper. Then trace and cut eight of the smaller of the two interior panels from the same color. Next, trace and cut eight of the larger of the two interior panels from a shade of craft paper that is darker than the base door, but the same tone.

STEP 6 To create Boo's door, trace and cut a base door shape from a sheet of light pink craft paper. Then trace and cut two of the smaller of the two arch-shaped interior panels from the same color. Also trace and cut two of the smaller of the two rectangular interior panels from the same color. Next, trace and cut two of the larger of the two arch-shaped interior panels from a sheet of dark pink craft paper. Also trace and cut out two of the larger of the rectangular interior panels from the dark pink paper.

STEP 7 Choose any combination of 8 doors and cut out the pieces required for each. To assemble the doors, begin by using the glue stick to apply adhesive to the back of the smaller, lighter-colored interior panel(s). Adhere atop the larger, darker-colored panel(s), centered in both dimensions. Apply adhesive to the back of the assembled darker-colored panel(s) and adhere atop the lighter-colored base door, spaced evenly.

STEP 8 For a double-panel door, situate the panels so that their long dimensions are perpendicular to the base door's long dimension. Position the top panel equidistant from the top edge of the door and the middle of the door, and position the bottom panel equidistant from the bottom edge of the door and the middle of the door. Both panels should be centered right-to-left. For a triple-panel door, situate the panels so that their long dimensions are perpendicular

to the base door's long dimension. Adhere one panel centered in each third of the base door. For an eight-panel door, imagine that the door is divided into two columns and four rows and adhere one panel centered in each imaginary box. For Boo's door, adhere the two arch-shaped panels to the top portion of the door, with their long dimensions parallel to the long dimension of the base door. Adhere the two rectangular panels to the bottom portion of the door, with their longer dimensions parallel to the long dimension of the base door. Finish Boo's door by adhering a few flower-shaped stickers to the bottom portion.

STEP 9 Once all the doors are assembled, use a toothpick to apply tacky glue to the back of a button. Adhere the button "doorknob" to the right side of a door. Repeat with remaining doors.

STEP 10 If making a garland, measure out a 48-inch length of thin ribbon. Leaving about 6 inches of ribbon free at each end, attach doors to the ribbon using packing tape, placing doors about 1 inch apart and taping the ribbon along the back of each door about 1/2 inch from the top.

STEP 11 If making invitations, cut a piece of card stock that is the same height and double the width of the base door. Fold the card stock in half and glue the door to the front of it. On the inside of the card, write "You're invited to a *Monsters* party!" followed by the party details.

SULLEY DRINK COASTERS

MAKES 6 COASTERS

MATERIALS

- SULLEY DRINK COASTERS TEMPLATE (P. 168)
- 1 (9 IN BY 12 IN) SHEET SOFT BLUE OR TURQUOISE CRAFT FOAM
- LILAC ACRYLIC CRAFT PAINT

TOOLS:

- SCISSORS
- PENCIL
- WAX PAPER OR NEWSPAPER
- PAPER PLATE
- SYNTHETIC CRAFT SPONGE

NOTE > The materials can be scaled up for the number of guests invited to your party.

During his tenure at Monsters, Inc., Sulley has some impressive achievements: he earns the ranking of top scarer, producing the most potent screams to power Monstropolis, and he—along with his best friend Mike Wazowski—discovers that children's laughter is actually more powerful than screams. These Sulley-inspired coasters will keep monsters and children from leaving unwanted marks on the coffee table and can be given out as party favors.

INSTRUCTIONS

STEP 1 Using the Sulley Drink Coasters template on page 168, make a photocopy enlarging it 200 percent. Carefully cut out the shape—this will be your master template.

STEP 2 Use the template to trace and cut out 6 coasters from the turquoise craft foam.

STEP 3 Spread out wax paper or old newspaper to protect your work surface. Pour a little of the lilac paint onto a paper plate. Tear off a piece of the craft sponge 1 to 1½ inches wide. Dip in the paint and create three or four randomly placed spots on each coaster. Let the paint dry completely (time will vary depending on temperature and humidity). Once the paint is dry, apply a second coat directly on top of the first round of spots. Allow the paint to dry completely before using or handing out to guests.

MIKE WAZOWSKI SPOON PUPPETS

MAKES 12 SPOON PUPPETS

MAKES 12 SPOON PUPPETS

MATERIALS

- MIKE WAZOWSKI SPOON PUPPET TEMPLATE (P. 168)
- 12 WOODEN SPOONS WITH HANDLES OF VARYING LENGTHS
- GREEN ACRYLIC CRAFT PAINT
- 1 (9 IN BY 12 IN) SHEET WHITE HEAVYWEIGHT CRAFT PAPER OR (8½ IN BY 11 IN) CARD STOCK (WILL MAKE 12 EYE WHITES)
- 1 (9 IN BY 12 IN) SHEET BLUE HEAVYWEIGHT CRAFT PAPER OR (8½ IN BY 11 IN) CARD STOCK (WILL MAKE 20 IRISES)
- 1 (9 IN BY 12 IN) SHEET BLACK HEAVYWEIGHT CRAFT PAPER OR (8½ IN BY 11 IN) CARD STOCK (WILL MAKE 30 PUPILS)
- WHITE ACRYLIC CRAFT PAINT
- JAR OR SMALL VASE
- DRIED BEANS

TOOLS:

- SYNTHETIC CRAFT SPONGE
- SCISSORS
- PENCIL
- GLUE STICK
- TOOTHPICK
- SMALL, STIFF PAINTBRUSH
- TACKY GLUE
- SMALL FOAM OR SOFT PAINTBRUSH
- DECOUPAGE SEALER (SUCH AS MOD PODGE®)

NOTE → The materials can be scaled up for the number of guests invited to your party.

While Mike Wazowski might not be the scariest-looking monster, his determination to be a scarer makes up for his lack of natural fearsomeness. His rise to scaredom isn't smooth, but with some help from his friend Sulley, he reaches his goal. To make this combination centerpiece and favor, all that's needed is an assortment of wooden spoons, acrylic paint, and an "eye" for detail.

INSTRUCTIONS

STEP 1 Use a piece of synthetic craft sponge and green acrylic paint to paint the wooden spoons, making sure to cover them completely. Let dry.

STEP 2 While spoons are drying, using the Mike Wazowski Spoon Puppet template on page 168, make a photocopy enlarging it 200 percent. Carefully cut out all of the shapes—this is your master template.

STEP 3 Trace the eye white onto a sheet of white heavyweight craft paper or card stock, making one eye white per spoon. Cut out and set aside.

STEP 4 Trace the iris onto a sheet of blue heavyweight craft paper or card stock, making one iris per spoon. Cut out and set aside.

STEP 5 Trace the pupil onto a sheet of black heavyweight craft paper or card stock, making one pupil per spoon. Cut out and set aside.

STEP 6 To assemble the eyes, apply glue to the back of a black pupil and adhere it to the center of a blue iris. Then apply glue to the back of the iris and adhere it to the center of a white circle. Use the tip of a toothpick to apply a tiny spot of white paint to the upper right edge of each pupil. Allow the eyes to dry completely.

STEP 7 Once the eyes and spoons have dried, use a small, stiff paintbrush to apply tacky glue to the back of an assembled eye. Adhere it in the center of the well of a wooden spoon.

To seal the eye, apply a layer of decoupage sealer with a small foam or soft paintbrush, coating the eye completely. Once all the eyes have been applied and sealed, let the spoons dry.

STEP 8 To display the spoons as a centerpiece, fill a clear class jar or vase with dried beans. Stick the spoon handles into the beans and arrange with the eyes facing out. Spoons can later be sent home with children as party favors.

RANDALL BOGGS BLUEBERRY SMOOTHIES

MAKES 8 5-OUNCE SMOOTHIES

MATERIALS

- RANDALL BOGGS CUP COVERS TEMPLATE (P. 168)
- 2 (9 IN BY 12 IN) SHEETS PURPLE HEAVYWEIGHT CRAFT PAPER
- 1 (9 IN BY 12 IN) SHEET WHITE HEAVYWEIGHT CRAFT PAPER
- 1 (9 IN BY 12 IN) SHEET GREEN HEAVYWEIGHT CRAFT PAPER
- 1 (9 IN BY 12 IN) SHEET BLACK HEAVYWEIGHT CRAFT PAPER
- 4 (9 IN BY 12 IN) SELF-ADHESIVE LAMINATING SHEETS (2 SHEETS FOR EVERY 6 CUP COVERS)
- 8 FLEXIBLE GREEN DRINKING STRAWS
- 8 GLASSES
- TRACING PAPER (OPTIONAL)

INGREDIENTS:

- 1⅔ C MILK
- 1¼ C FROZEN BLUEBERRIES
- 1 LARGE BANANA, SLICED
- 1¼ C VANILLA FROZEN YOGURT
- 2 TBSP MAPLE SYRUP

TOOLS:

- SCISSORS
- PENCIL
- GLUE STICK
- RULER
- CRAFT KNIFE
- BLENDER

When Mike Wazowski first makes the acquaintance of Randall "Randy" Boggs at Monsters University, they are both enrolled in the scaring program. If only Mike had known that Randall would later become his chief rival at Monsters, Inc., maybe he wouldn't have been so willing to help the creepy purple fiend! While they definitely aren't scary, these smoothies share two important qualities with Randall: they are purple and they have the tendency to disappear!

INSTRUCTIONS

STEP 1 Using the Randall Boggs Cup Covers template on page 168, make a photocopy enlarging it 200 percent. Carefully cut out all of the shapes—this is your master template.

STEP 2 Trace the glass frame circle template piece onto a sheet of purple heavyweight craft paper. You will need one frame circle for each cup cover. Cut out the circles and set aside.

STEP 3 Trace the eye white template piece onto a sheet of white heavyweight craft paper, tracing one eye white per cup cover. Cut out and set aside.

STEP 4 Trace the iris template piece onto a sheet of green heavyweight craft paper, tracing one iris per cup cover. Cut out and set aside.

STEP 5 Trace the pupil template piece onto a sheet of black heavyweight craft paper, tracing one pupil per cup cover. Cut out and set aside.

STEP 6 To assemble the cup covers, apply glue to the back of a black pupil and adhere it to the center of a green iris. Then apply glue to the back of the iris and adhere it to the center of a white circle. Finally, apply glue to the back of the white and adhere it to the center of the purple frame circle. Allow cup covers to dry completely.

STEP 7 To protect each cup cover, cut two 4-inch squares from a laminating sheet. Remove the backing from one of the squares and place it on your work surface sticky-side up. Carefully place the cup cover on top of the laminating square, making sure it's centered. Remove the backing from the second square of laminating material and place it, sticky-side down, on top of the cup cover, so that the edges of both laminating squares are flush. Place the wide, flat side of a ruler on top of the laminated cup cover, and press down on the ruler, moving it across the surface to smoothly seal the layers together. Use scissors to trim the excess laminating material, leaving a ¼-inch border of laminating material around the edge of the purple paper.

STEP 8 To create the holes for the straws, use a craft knife to cut a small X through the center of each pupil, making sure to cut through all layers of lamination and paper. Insert the bottom end of a green flexible straw through the X-shaped hole in the cup cover, and slide the cover up to the flexible portion of the straw.

STEP 9 To make the smoothies, combine the milk, blueberries, banana, frozen yogurt, and maple syrup in a blender. Puree until the mixture is thick and creamy. Divide among eight glasses and insert a straw and cup cover into each glass. Serve immediately.

TERRY AND TERRI TERRIFYING FLATBREAD SANDWICHES

MAKES 8 SANDWICHES
(4 TERRYS AND 4 TERRIS)

- TERRY AND TERRI TERRIFYING FLATBREAD SANDWICHES TEMPLATE (P. 168)

INGREDIENTS:

- 2 (10 IN) ROUND SUN-DRIED TOMATO FLATBREADS
- SMALL GREEN BELL PEPPER
- 4 PITTED BLACK OLIVES
- 1 (8 OZ) CONTAINER OF WHIPPED CREAM CHEESE
- 1 SLICE DELI HAM
- 1 SLICE FRESH MOZZARELLA (ABOUT 1/8 INCH THICK)
- 4 ALMOND SLICES (1 SLICE FOR EACH TERRY)
- 8 CASHEW HALVES (2 HALVES FOR EACH TERRI)

TOOLS:

- SCISSORS
- 1 (2¼ TO 2⅜ IN) ROUND COOKIE OR FONDANT CUTTER
- 1 (1 IN AT BASE) ROUND METAL PASTRY BAG TIP
- KITCHEN KNIFE
- 1 (⅝ IN) ROUND FONDANT CUTTER
- 1 (⅜ IN AT TIP) ROUND METAL PASTRY BAG TIP
- BUTTER KNIFE

Terry and Terri are attached at the hip—literally. A two-headed monster with four arms and seven tentacles, Terry and Terri don't agree on much, except that they would love to become scarers someday. To make sandwiches in honor of these Oozma Kappa brothers, fill sun-dried tomato flatbread circles with veggie cream cheese and then top them with cheese-and-olive eyes. Your child's guests are sure to agree; these sandwiches are terrifyingly tasty!

INSTRUCTIONS

STEP 1 Using the Terry and Terri Terrifying Flatbread Sandwiches template on page 168, make a photocopy enlarging it 200 percent. Carefully cut out the shapes—this is your master template.

STEP 2 For each pair of Terry and Terri sandwiches, use the large cookie or fondant cutter to cut four circles from the sun-dried tomato flatbread (one Terri and one Terry).

STEP 3 Using the Terry template piece as reference for placement, use the 1-inch round metal pastry bag tip to cut a 1-inch hole for Terry's eye in one of the flatbread circles.

STEP 4 Using the Terri template piece as reference for placement, use the round metal pastry bag tip to cut a 1-inch hole for Terri's eye in a second flatbread circle.

STEP 5 Place the Terry template atop the first flatbread circle and use a kitchen knife to cut a hole in the flatbread for his mouth opening. Set aside.

STEP 6 Place the Terri template atop the second flatbread circle and use a kitchen knife to cut along his mouth line. Set aside.

STEP 7 To create the eyes, use a kitchen knife to slice off one of the sides of the green bell pepper. Use the 5/8-inch round fondant cutter to cut two circles of green pepper. Then use the 3/8-inch round metal pastry bag tip to cut a 3/8-inch hole in the center of each green pepper circle. Slice the sides off a large black olive. Use the same 3/8-inch round pastry bag tip to cut a pupil from each black olive slice. Insert a black olive circle into the hole in each green pepper iris. Set aside.

STEP 8 Place the Terry mouth template piece atop a slice of ham and use a kitchen knife to cut out the shape. Set aside.

STEP 9 Use a butter knife to spread cream cheese atop the two remaining whole flatbread circles. Top one with the Terry flatbread circle, and the other with the Terri flatbread circle. Gently press a pepper-and-olive eye into the center of each eye hole. Insert Terry's ham mouth into the mouth hole in the flatbread.

STEP 10 If desired, use a toothpick to place a tiny dot of cream cheese at the right edge of each pupil to create an eye glint.

STEP 11 Place the Terri eyelid template piece atop a scrap piece of flatbread and cut out the shape. Spread a small amount of cream cheese on the back of the flatbread eyelid, and then position over the top half of Terri's eye.

STEP 12 To create the teeth, use a kitchen knife to cut four rectangles from the mozzarella slice, about 1/4 inch wide and 3/8 inch long. Use the 3/8-inch round pastry bag tip to cut two circles from the mozzarella slice.

STEP 13 Position two of the larger, rectangular teeth in Terri's mouth by tucking them under the upper lip of his mouth slit. Position the remaining two larger, rectangular teeth in Terri's mouth atop the ham, tucking the top edges under the left side of the upper lip. Place the three circular mozzarella teeth to the right of the two larger rectangular teeth, tucking the top edges under the right side of the upper lip.

STEP 14 To add the horns, tuck an almond slice, face up, in between the layers of flatbread at the top of Terry's head. Tuck a cashew half in between the layers of flatbread on either side of Terri's eye. Refrigerate until ready to serve.

MIKE WAZOWSKI CUPCAKES

MATERIALS

- 1 (24 OZ) PACKAGE WHITE, READY-TO-USE FONDANT
- GREEN FOOD COLORING
- BLUE FOOD COLORING
- BLACK FOOD COLORING
- POWDERED SUGAR, FOR ROLLING
- 24 WHITE SUGAR PEARLS
- FAVORITE RECIPE FOR 24 CUPCAKES, PREPARED IN GREEN CUPCAKE LINERS, ICED WITH GREEN FROSTING
- SLICED ALMONDS (48 SLICES)

TOOLS:

- KITCHEN GLOVES (OPTIONAL)
- PLASTIC WRAP
- WAX PAPER
- ROLLING PIN
- 1 (2¼ IN) CIRCULAR FONDANT CUTTER
- 1 (1⅜ IN) CIRCULAR FONDANT CUTTER
- 1 (⅝ IN) CIRCULAR FONDANT CUTTER
- PUSHPIN
- TOOTHPICK

Energetic, dedicated, and studious, Mike Wazowski begins his freshman year at Monsters University with his eye on the prize: a degree in scaring. While his plans don't turn out quite like he had hoped, that doesn't stop him from getting his just desserts. Speaking of desserts, these Mike Wazowski cupcakes—topped with green and white fondant—are the eye-deal finale for a *Monsters*-themed feast.

INSTRUCTIONS

STEP 1 Separate the fondant into two equal halves (each about 12 ounces). Add green food coloring to one half and knead the fondant (wearing kitchen gloves is a good idea) until the color is uniform and the desired shade is achieved. Wrap tightly in plastic wrap and set aside.

STEP 2 Of the remaining portion of white fondant, reserve two thirds of it and wrap it tightly in plastic wrap. Set aside. Divide the remaining third into two equal parts. Add blue food coloring to one part and knead until the color is uniform and the desired shade is achieved. Wrap tightly in plastic wrap and set aside. Add black food coloring to the remaining fondant and knead until the color is uniform and the desired shade is achieved. Wrap tightly in plastic wrap and set aside.

STEP 3 Cover the work surface with a sheet of wax paper and sprinkle with powdered sugar. Unwrap green fondant and roll out to a ⅜-inch thickness, dusting the fondant and rolling pin with additional powdered sugar if it begins to stick. Use the 2¼-inch circular fondant cutter to cut out twenty-four circles of green fondant. Place circles on a separate piece of wax paper and set aside.

STEP 4 Cover the work surface with a new sheet of wax paper sprinkled with powdered sugar and roll out white fondant to a ⅜-inch thickness, dusting the fondant and rolling pin with additional powdered sugar if it begins to stick. Use the 1⅜-inch circular fondant cutter to cut out twenty-four circles of white fondant. Use the same fondant cutter to cut a hole in the center of each green fondant circle. Carefully insert one white fondant circle into the hole in each green fondant circle.

STEP 5 Cover the work surface with a new sheet of wax paper sprinkled with powdered sugar and roll out blue fondant to a ⅜-inch thickness, dusting the fondant and rolling pin with additional powdered sugar if it begins to stick. Use the ⅝-inch circular fondant cutter to cut out twenty-four circles of blue fondant. Use the same fondant cutter to cut a hole in the center of each white fondant circle. Carefully insert one blue fondant circle into the hole in each white fondant circle. You should now have twenty-four green fondant circles with white eyes and blue irises.

STEP 6 To make the pupils for the eyes, roll twenty-four tiny balls of black fondant about ⅛ inch in diameter. Flatten the balls slightly. Use the flat end of a pushpin to create a shallow depression in the center of each blue iris. Gently press one black pupil into each depression.

STEP 7 To add glints to the eyes, place a sugar pearl atop the upper right edge of each pupil. Use a toothpick to gently press the sugar pearl into the fondant so it stays in place.

STEP 8 Prepare your favorite recipe for twenty-four cupcakes in green cupcake liners. Once cupcakes are completely cool, frost with green icing. Top each frosted cupcake with an assembled fondant eye, pressing down just slightly so it adheres to the frosting.

STEP 9 Finally, to create Mike's horns, insert an almond slice, face up, underneath the outside edge of the green fondant nearest to the sugar pearl, pushing it in about halfway. Insert a second almond slice about 1 inch to the left of the first. Keep in a cool, dry place until ready to serve.

SULLEY'S DORM PARTY POPCORN FAVORS

MAKES 8 BAGS OF POPCORN

MATERIALS

- BLUE CRAFT PAPER
- PURPLE CRAFT PAPER
- 8 (4 IN BY 9 IN) PLASTIC TREAT BAGS
- 8 (12 IN) LENGTHS NARROW BLUE RIBBON
- 8 (12 IN) LENGTHS NARROW PURPLE RIBBON

INGREDIENTS:

- 2 (3½ OZ) BAGS MICROWAVE POPCORN
- 1 STICK (8 TBSP) BUTTER, DIVIDED
- 6 TBSP LIGHT CORN SYRUP, DIVIDED
- 1 C SUGAR, DIVIDED
- 1 (3 OZ) BOX BLUE (BERRY-FLAVORED) GELATIN DESSERT MIX
- 1 (3 OZ) BOX PURPLE (GRAPE-FLAVORED) GELATIN DESSERT MIX

TOOLS:

- 2 LARGE BAKING SHEETS
- PARCHMENT PAPER OR WAXED PAPER
- LARGE BOWL
- MEDIUM HEAVY-BOTTOMED SAUCEPAN
- LONG-HANDLED WOODEN SPOON
- SCISSORS
- GLUE STICK
- CRAFT KNIFE

The son of legendary scarer Bill Sullivan, James P. Sullivan expects to be an instant success when he enrolls in the scaring program at Monsters University. After all, he sure does look the part! To make popcorn party favors that look just like Sulley, coat popped kernels with blue and purple gelatin dessert mix and you've got a scare-tastic treat to send home with your guests.

INSTRUCTIONS

STEP 1 Preheat oven to 250°F. Line two large baking sheets with parchment or waxed paper.

STEP 2 Cook one bag of microwave popcorn according to the package directions and then pour into a large bowl.

STEP 3 In a saucepan over medium heat, combine 4 tablespoons butter, 3 tablespoons corn syrup, and ½ cup sugar. Add blue gelatin, and simmer over low heat for 5 minutes, stirring constantly with a wooden spoon. Mixture will be extremely hot.

STEP 4 Drizzle gelatin mixture over popped corn and stir with a wooden spoon to coat the kernels as evenly as possible without crushing the popcorn. Turn the coated popcorn onto one of the lined baking sheets. Bake for 8 to 10 minutes or until crisp, checking often to make sure it doesn't start to brown. Remove from the oven and cool completely.

STEP 5 Repeat steps 2 through 4 with the second bag of popcorn and the purple gelatin.

STEP 6 Once both flavors of popcorn are completely cool, break larger clumps into small pieces.

STEP 7 Fill the plastic treat bags with popcorn, alternating colors to create patches of blue and purple. Tie off bags with a pair of ribbons, one purple and one blue.

STEP 8 To make decorative Monsters University pennants, cut small, slender triangles from the purple craft paper. Cut slightly smaller slender triangles from the blue craft paper. Glue a blue triangle in the center of a purple triangle and let dry. Use the craft knife to cut a tiny hole in one corner of each pennant. Thread one of the ribbon ends through the hole in the pennant, and then tie a knot in the end of the ribbon to prevent the pennant from slipping off.

STOMP & SAVE!

GAME FOR 10–25 GUESTS

MATERIALS

- ❤ DIFFERENT COLORED BALLOONS
- ❤ STRING

This one's a classic! We all know how dangerous children can be. Well, except for Boo, of course. So let's pretend that Boo is a balloon that needs saving. She is attached to you. But the other balloons are the real monsters. So it's a question of stomping and saving!

INSTRUCTIONS

STEP 1   Inflate as many balloons as needed for the game.

STEP 2   Fix one end of a string to a balloon and the other to a guest playing the game.

STEP 3   Each guest believes that his balloon is Boo but the other balloons are monsters. Boo needs saving, the others need stomping!

STEP 4   The mission is to stomp out all the other balloons and save yours. The last one left with his balloon wins.

MONSTER'S SCAVANGER HUNT

GAME FOR 10-25 GUESTS

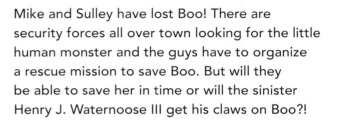

MATERIALS

- 5-6 DIFFERENT RIDDLES
- 5-6 DIFFERENT CLUES
- COLORED PAPER
- A PICTURE OF BOO

Mike and Sulley have lost Boo! There are security forces all over town looking for the little human monster and the guys have to organize a rescue mission to save Boo. But will they be able to save her in time or will the sinister Henry J. Waternoose III get his claws on Boo?!

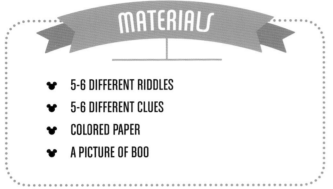

INSTRUCTIONS

STEP 1 Split the guests into two opposing groups. Group One is Mike and Sulley's. Group Two is the security forces. Both groups want to find Boo as soon as possible!

STEP 2 Before the party, start planning the hunt for Boo in detail. Plant at least 5 clues or riddles in various locations arround the neighborhood. The difficulty level can vary but try to keep the locations in the near vicinity of your house or apartment. Be sure to choose locations that most of the guests recognize.

STEP 3 You can decorate the clues in various colored paper, but be sure to assign different colors to each group. That way there is no confusion if both groups get to the same place at the same time.

STEP 4 The clues or riddles can be based on information from the animations Monsters Inc. or Monsters Academy.
Here are a few helpful suggestions:
(Note: Where there is a riddle one adult must be present to say the riddle and receive an answer.)

Riddle 1: Who is Mike's best friend?
Answer: Sulley.
Riddle 2: Who is Mike's girlfriend?
Answer: Celia.
Riddle 3: Why are the monsters afraid of little children?
Answer: Because they think they are toxic!
Riddle 4: Who is Mike's worst enemy?
Answer: Randall.

Contestants must answer these, or other, questions correctly. An adult then gives the group directions to the next location. If they do not have the answer they must wait for 1 minute before continuing.

Clues: When contestants arrive at a location they will find a note or a package in their team colors. There they will get clues or instructions to the next location.
Note: The person throwing the party has to be sure every instruction or clue is based on the contestants knowledge of the surrounding neighborhood.

STEP 5 The fist team to find Boo wins.

WRECK-IT RALPH
PARTY

When *Wreck-It Ralph* hit theaters in 2012, the film's hero—despite actually being a "bad guy"—won over viewers with his determination, goofy grin, and tender heart. As Ralph explores the worlds contained within the games of Litwak's Arcade, he learns several important truths about himself and even makes some friends along the way, including the indomitable soldier Calhoun from *Hero's Duty*; the eponymous hammer-holding hero from his native game, *Fix-It Felix, Jr.*; and the adorable glitch from *Sugar Rush*, Vanellope von Schweetz.

All of Ralph's friends and their respective games are represented in this pixilated party, which features crafts, activities, and recipes that will score big points with kids who love gaming, the characters from *Wreck-It Ralph*, and the movie's message: no matter what situation you find yourself in, you can rise above your circumstances and become a hero. Start by spreading the word with *Fix-It Felix, Jr.* arcade game invitations. Once the guests arrive, dial up the fun with the "I'm Gonna Wreck It!" Penthouse Piñata and Pin the Hammer on Fix-It Felix, Jr. After partaking in the party activities, kids are sure to have built up a hero-sized appetite, so refuel them with Pile-of-Bricks Finger Sandwiches and *Hero's Duty* Medal Pizza. Then it's time for a sweet—and interactive!—ending with Vanellope's Race Car Brownies.

FIX-IT FELIX, JR. ARCADE GAME INVITATIONS

MATERIALS

- 1 (12 IN BY 12 IN) SHEET BRIGHT BLUE CARD STOCK
- 1 (12 IN BY 12 IN) SHEET BRIGHT YELLOW CARD STOCK
- 1 (12 IN BY 12 IN) SHEET BLACK CARD STOCK
- RED AND ORANGE ¼-INCH "BUTTON CANDY" STICK-ON JELLIES
- GLITTERY ¼-INCH STAR-SHAPED STICKERS IN A VARIETY OF COLORS
- ENVELOPES (OPTIONAL)

TOOLS:

- PENCIL
- RULER
- SCISSORS
- PAPER CUTTER (OPTIONAL)
- GLUE TAPE (DOUBLE-SIDED ADHESIVE) APPLICATOR WITH NARROW TIP OR GLUE STICK
- ULTRA FINE POINT BLACK PERMANENT MARKER
- FINE POINT SILVER PAINT MARKER
- ULTRA FINE POINT RED PERMANENT MARKER

NOTE The materials can be scaled up for the number of guests invited to your party.

The Fix-It Felix, Jr. arcade game is where the action of the film begins, so it's a fitting inspiration for these invitations. No golden hammer needed—just some card stock, permanent markers, and a silver paint marker.

INSTRUCTIONS

STEP 1 Using a pencil, ruler, and scissors—or a paper cutter if preferred—measure and cut out a 7-by-3½-inch rectangle from the bright blue card stock.

STEP 2 From the sheet of bright yellow card stock, cut out a ⅞-by-3⅜-inch rectangle and a 2⅝-inch square.

STEP 3 From the sheet of black card stock, cut out a 1⅞-inch square, then use scissors to round the corners. Also measure and cut out a trapezoid measuring 3⅜ inches wide at the top, 2⅝ inches wide across the bottom, and ⅜ inch tall. (The line you'll trace for the bottom of the trapezoid will begin ⅜ inch inside of the ends of the line you traced for the top.)

STEP 4 Using the glue tape or glue stick, apply adhesive all around the edges of the yellow rectangle. Place it horizontally, just below the top of the blue rectangle, and press to adhere.

STEP 5 Apply adhesive to the back of the black trapezoid and place it, longer side at the top, just underneath and flush to the yellow rectangle. Press to adhere.

STEP 6 Apply adhesive to the back of the yellow square and place it flush to the underside of the black trapezoid. Press to adhere.

STEP 7 Apply adhesive to the back of the black rounded square and situate in the middle of the yellow square. Press to adhere.

STEP 8 Using a ruler and ultra fine point black permanent marker, draw a horizontal line $5/8$ inch below the bottom of the yellow square. It should stop $1/8$ inch from the outside edges of the blue card stock.

STEP 9 Draw another horizontal line $7/8$ inch below the line drawn in step 8, again stopping $1/8$ inch from the outside edges of the blue card stock.

STEP 10 Draw two vertical lines connecting the ends of the two horizontal lines made in steps 8 and 9.

STEP 11 Line up your ruler with the bottom left corner of the yellow square and the top left corner of the rectangle you've just drawn. Draw a diagonal line connecting the points.

STEP 12 Repeat step 11 on the right side of the yellow square.

STEP 13 Using a scrap of the yellow card stock, cut out the knob of a joy stick, color it red with the red marker, and adhere using glue tape or glue stick to the trapezoid you've just drawn. Use the black marker to draw the joystick's stem.

STEP 14 To the right of the joystick, adhere four "button candy" stick-on jellies—two of each color—for the arcade game's buttons.

STEP 15 With the silver paint marker, write "High Scorer:" followed by "(Birthday Boy)" or "(Birthday Girl)" and your child's name on the black rounded square screen in the center of the invitation.

STEP 16 With the black marker, write "You're invited to a" across the top of the yellow rectangle. Use the red marker to write "WRECK-IT RALPH" in all-capital letters, then use the black marker to write "party!"

STEP 17 Using the black marker, fill in any remaining information at the bottom of the invitation, including the location of the party, the date, time, RSVP information, and other pertinent details.

STEP 18 Place glittery star stickers on either side of "You're invited to a" as well as on either side of the child's name and in each of the four corners of the yellow square.

"I'M GONNA WRECK IT!" PENTHOUSE PIÑATA

MAKES 1 PIÑATA

MATERIALS

- 1 (16 IN TALL BY 10 IN WIDE BY 10 IN DEEP) CARDBOARD BOX
- 1 (18 IN) LENGTH BRAIDED FRAMING WIRE
- 6 (9 IN BY 12 IN) SHEETS RED CONSTRUCTION PAPER
- 2 (9 IN BY 12 IN) SHEETS BEIGE CONSTRUCTION PAPER
- 4 (9 IN BY 12 IN) SHEETS WHITE CONSTRUCTION PAPER
- 1 (9 IN BY 12 IN) SHEET BLUE CONSTRUCTION PAPER
- 2 (9 IN BY 12 IN) SHEETS GREEN CONSTRUCTION PAPER
- "I'M GONNA WRECK IT!" PENTHOUSE PIÑATA RALPH TEMPLATE (P. 171)
- "I'M GONNA WRECK IT!" PENTHOUSE PIÑATA FELIX TEMPLATE (P. 171)
- 1 (5 YD) LENGTH NYLON CORD
- BLINDFOLD

TOOLS:
- RULER
- PENCIL
- UTILITY KNIFE
- PACKING TAPE
- AWL
- HAMMER
- SCISSORS
- GLUE TAPE (DOUBLE-SIDED ADHESIVE) APPLICATOR OR GLUE STICK
- HOT GLUE GUN

Once you've made this Penthouse Piñata and filled it with goodies, party guests can take turns trying to "wreck" it, just like Ralph does. To take the authenticity a step further, you can even purchase a pair of boxing gloves and allow little gamers to jab away!

INSTRUCTIONS

STEP 1   Begin by making sure your cardboard box is taped securely and thoroughly at all seams except for at one narrow end (this will become the "roof" of the building). If you cannot find a ready-made cardboard box at the specified dimensions, you can easily create one from a larger cardboard box. Use a ruler and pencil to measure four panels that are 16 inches tall and 10 inches wide, and two 10-inch square panels. Cut the panels using a utility knife (and use the ruler as a guide to ensure straight edges). Then tape the panels together, allowing a little space between the pieces so the taped corners can bend.

STEP 2   If your cardboard box has only one 10-by-10-inch flap at the top, set the box on its side with the top flap lying open. You may want to place the flap on top of some extra pieces of cardboard or foam so the tip of the awl doesn't dent your work surface. Using the awl and the hammer, punch two holes along the center line of the top flap, about 3 inches apart from each other. Make sure to hammer the point of the awl all the way through the cardboard. If your box has two 5-by-10-inch flaps, punch one hole in each flap, in the center, about 1½ inches from the edge of each flap. Loop the piece of braided framing wire through the holes and twist the last 2 inches of one end around the last 2 inches of the other end. The twisting should be done on the underside of the cardboard flap so it doesn't show. Now use the packing tape to join the roof flap(s) securely to the sides of the building. It has to hold up under the weight of the goodies you'll put inside!

STEP 3 To create the floors of the building, use a ruler, pencil, and scissors to measure and cut out 10-by-4-inch rectangles of construction paper. You will need twelve red floors and four beige floors to cover the entire piñata. (Each sheet of construction paper can accommodate two floors.)

STEP 4 To cut out windows from the white construction paper, measure columns that are 1½ inches wide, and then cut each column into six 2-inch segments. You should be able to get twenty-four 1½-by-2-inch windows out of each sheet of construction paper. There are nineteen windows per side of the building, so you'll need seventy-six windows total.

STEP 5 To create the doors, measure a column on the blue construction paper that is 2 inches wide. Cut it at 3-inch intervals, resulting in four 2-by-3-inch doors. Use your scissors to round off the tops of the doors.

STEP 6 For the roof, measure and cut two 5-by-10-inch rectangles from the sheets of green construction paper.

STEP 7 Once all your pieces are cut, begin assembling the floors by using your glue tape or glue stick to adhere five windows, equally spaced, onto each red rectangle. To create the beige floors, which are the ground floor of the building, first glue a blue door in the center, then glue two windows on each side. Once all sixteen floors are assembled, plug in your hot glue gun.

STEP 8 Starting with the ground level, flip over one of the beige floors and apply a thin bead of hot glue around the perimeter to the back. Carefully position at the base on one side of the cardboard box. Apply glue to the back of a red floor and position above and flush to the ground floor. Repeat with two additional red floors.

STEP 9 Repeat step 7 on the other three sides of the piñata.

STEP 10 For the roof, glue the two green rectangles on either side of the hanging wire to cover the top end of the cardboard box.

STEP 11 Using the Ralph and Felix templates on page 171, make a photocopy enlarging it 200 percent. Carefully cut out the 1½-by-2-inch rectangle containing Felix and, using the glue tape or glue stick, adhere it on top of one of the windows on the front of your building (second or third floor is best). Carefully cut out the image of Ralph and, using the glue tape or glue stick, adhere it to the ground floor on the front of your building.

STEP 12 Now it's time to cut a loading port in your piñata. This can be in the roof or on one of the sides of the penthouse, depending on your preference. Use a utility knife to make two parallel cuts in the cardboard, about 3 inches apart, each about 3 inches long. Make one more cut connecting the ends of the first two cuts. Pull open the flap and fill the piñata with toys, candy, or a combination of both. Now tape the flap back up again and your piñata is ready to go!

CANDY CANE TREE CENTERPIECE

MAKES 1 CENTERPIECE

MATERIALS

- 1 (12 IN BY 18 IN) SHEET RED CRAFT FOAM
- 1 (3⅞ IN BY 14⅝ IN) FOAM CONE
- 1 (6 IN TO 8 IN) CIRCULAR OR SQUARE PIECE HARDWOOD, PLYWOOD, OR PARTICLE BOARD
- 7 TO 8 FT WHITE SATIN RIBBON, ⅝ IN WIDE
- 22 CANDY CANES, WRAPPERS ON

TOOLS:
- PENCIL
- SCISSORS
- PRECISION UTILITY KNIFE
- RED DUCT TAPE
- HOT GLUE GUN

After Ralph crash-lands in the world of *Sugar Rush*, his *Hero's Duty* medal is flung into one of the branches of a candy cane tree. As he climbs the tree to retrieve the medal, he meets Vanellope von Schweetz—and discovers that double-striped branches disappear when you grab onto them! The branches of this candy cane tree centerpiece will disappear at the end of your child's party, too—that is, when the guests take them home as favors!

INSTRUCTIONS

STEP 1 Wrap the sheet of craft foam around the foam cone, mark off the dimensions with a pencil, and then cut with scissors to make a flattened cone shape that will fully cover the foam cone.

STEP 2 Use the precision utility knife to cut twenty-two small, circular holes in the piece of craft foam. The holes should be spaced at random and just large enough to allow the stems of your candy canes to pass through.

STEP 3 Place the foam cone on the center of your piece of board and use several pieces of red duct tape to secure it. If they fan out in a star formation, they will look like the spreading roots of a tree.

STEP 4 Wrap the piece of craft foam around the foam cone and secure using either hot glue or additional red duct tape. Cut a small circular piece of red craft foam to cover the top of the cone and secure using hot glue or duct tape.

STEP 5 Starting at the base and gradually working your way up, wrap the white satin ribbon in a spiral around the cone, securing it with hot glue as you go and avoiding the holes cut in the craft foam. (If you have to cover a hole, you can cut a new hole just above or below it with the precision utility knife.)

STEP 6 Insert the candy canes into the holes, pushing them into the foam cone just far enough so that they won't shift or droop.

STEP 7 Display on the table during your child's party and encourage departing guests to take a candy cane as a party favor.

PIN THE HAMMER ON FIX-IT FELIX, JR.

······ MAKES 1 GAME ······

MATERIALS

- 1 (22 IN BY 28 IN) SHEET OF POSTER BOARD
- GOLDEN HAMMER TEMPLATE (P. 171)
- 1 (6 IN) SQUARE SHEET OF GOLD-FOIL CARD STOCK PER CHILD
- REMOVABLE MOUNTING PUTTY
- BLINDFOLD

TOOLS:

- PENCIL
- SET OF WASHABLE MARKERS IN A VARIETY OF COLORS
- ERASER
- RULER
- SCISSORS

The hero of Ralph's arcade game, Fix-It Felix, Jr., requires a special item to perform his handyman duties: a golden hammer. For this update of Pin the Tail on the Donkey, children will take turns pinning golden hammers on Felix, attempting to place their hammer in his right hand.

INSTRUCTIONS

STEP 1   Make a photocopy of the Felix outline on page 171, enlarging it 200 percent.

STEP 2   Selecting colors that match the image of Felix as closely as possible, color in the lines.

STEP 3   Using the hammer template on page 171, make a photocopy enlarging it 200 percent. Carefully cut out the hammer and trace it—with the head of the hammer facing right—onto the back of a sheet of gold-foil card stock. Cut out one gold foil hammer per child attending the party.

PIN THE HAMMER ON FIX-IT FELIX, JR.

HOW TO PLAY

When it's time to play, place a dime-sized piece of removable mounting putty on the back of each golden hammer. Place a quarter-sized piece of the putty in each corner on the back of the Felix poster board. Hang it up on a wall at the appropriate height for the children attending the party.

Blindfold the children in turn, hand them each a golden hammer, gently spin them around three times, and then direct them toward the Felix poster. Whichever child places his or her hammer closest to Felix's right hand wins a prize!

ENLARGE 200%

PILE OF BRICKS FINGER SANDWICHES

MAKES 8 SANDWICHES

INGREDIENTS

- 3 (9 IN) SUN-DRIED TOMATO OR RED PEPPER-FLAVORED WRAPS
- 16 LARGE SLICES DELI MEAT (HAM, TURKEY, ROAST BEEF, OR CHICKEN)
- 8 LARGE SLICES CHEESE (CHEDDAR, MUENSTER, PROVOLONE, OR MONTEREY JACK)
- MUSTARD OR MAYONNAISE

TOOLS:

- RULER
- SHARP KNIFE
- 1 (½ IN DIAMETER) CAP FROM A WASHABLE MARKER

Ralph lives (uncomfortably) on a hill of red bricks—by-products of his habit of wrecking the Niceland apartment building. These finger sandwiches can be made using brick-colored sun-dried tomato or red pepper flavored wraps and filled with any type of sliced meat and cheese. A vegetarian version could be made with veggies and cream cheese.

INSTRUCTIONS

STEP 1 Use a ruler and a sharp knife to cut five or six 2-by-4-inch rectangles out of each 9-inch tortilla. A total of sixteen rectangles are needed to make eight sandwiches. Set aside eight of the wrap rectangles. These are the bottom layers of the sandwiches.

STEP 2 Use the cap of a child's washable marker to cut three holes, evenly spaced vertically, along the center line of the remaining eight wrap rectangles. These are the top layers of the sandwiches.

STEP 3 Place one bottom-layer rectangle on your work surface. Apply a small amount of mustard or mayonnaise in the center of the rectangle. Layer with one slice of meat, a slice of cheese, and then another slice of meat. If the slices of meat and cheese are not large enough to span the entire surface of the wrap rectangle, two slices can be layered overlapping. Trim the edges of the meat and cheese to align with the edges of the bottom layer wrap rectangle.

STEP 4 Apply a small amount of mustard or mayonnaise to one of the top-layer rectangles and place (with the spread face down) on top of the sandwich.

STEP 5 Repeat steps 3 and 4 with the remaining sandwiches. Refrigerate until ready to serve.

HERO'S DUTY MEDAL PIZZA

MAKES 1 (13 IN) PIZZA

INGREDIENTS

- 1 (16 OZ) PACKAGE PREMADE PIZZA DOUGH
- 1 TO 2 TBSP FLOUR
- 1 C PIZZA SAUCE
- 1 C SHREDDED MOZZERELLA
- 1 C SHREDDED ITALIAN FIVE-CHEESE BLEND
- 1 (6 OZ) PACKAGE SLICED PEPPERONI
- 1 (2¼ OZ) CAN BLACK OLIVE SLICES

TOOLS:

- 1 (16 IN) ROUND NONSTICK PIZZA PAN
- SMALL BOWL
- PIZZA CUTTER

Tired of being the bad guy and repeatedly watching Fix-It Felix, Jr. win medals, Ralph becomes determined to win a medal of his own. He enters another arcade game called *Hero's Duty* and manages to attain a gold medal emblazoned with a star and the word hero. Awarding your birthday boy or girl with a *Hero's Duty* Medal Pizza is much easier than conquering a hoard of Cy-bugs!

INSTRUCTIONS

STEP 1 Preheat the oven to 450°F. Place dough on pizza pan. Sprinkle dough lightly with flour and spread, pressing gently with fingertips, into a 14-inch circle.

STEP 2 Spoon pizza sauce onto crust and spread to within an inch of the edge of the crust. In a small bowl, combine the two cheeses. Sprinkle evenly over the top of the pizza sauce.

STEP 3 Arrange slices of pepperoni, overlapping, in a star shape on top of the cheese.

STEP 4 Use black olive slices to spell out the word hero across the middle of the pepperoni star.

STEP 5 Place in oven and bake for 12 to 15 minutes, until crust is lightly browned and toppings are bubbling.

STEP 6 Using a pizza cutter, slice into eight wedges and serve.

VANELLOPE'S CHOCOLATE MASS

MAKES 1.5 LB CHOCOLATE MASS

INGREDIENTS

- 1 LB WHITE CHOCOLATE COATING
- 0.5 LB GLUCOSE

TOOLS:
- LARGE BOWL
- SPADE
- PLASTIC FILM

Vanellope von Schweetz is Ralph's best friend. She originally comes from the game Sugar Rush, a world filled with beautifull, delicious candy and cakes. Here below is one way to make a beautifull decoration with chocolate mass for any type of cake ... the Sugar Rush way!

INSTRUCTIONS

STEP 1 Melt white chocolate coating in a bowl over boiling water or in the microwave. Heat the coating for about a minute, stop and stir. Put it back in the microwave for about half a minute and stop again and stir. Repeat as needed to completely melt the coating.

STEP 2 Pour the glucose syrup into the melted chocolate coating and stir slowly together until the mass becomes like clay. Be careful not to stir to much and not to knead the clay like mass.

STEP 3 When the chocolate coating and glucose has become a dense mass it is placed on a half of a large piece of plastic wrap.

STEP 4 Fold the other half of the plastic wrap over the mass and roll it out with a roller or by hand.

STEP 5 Cool the mass in the fridge for at least two hours before it is used.

GOOD TO KNOW

• It is possible to color the chocolate mass with gel food color and powder food colors. May also use colored chocolate coating.

• The mass can keep for several months in the fridge.

• Remove the mass from the refrigerator and divide it into small units. The chocolate mass can be very stiff when taken from the fridge and difficult to knead all at once. Therefore you should knead each unit separately before adding it all in a big ball and knead together.

• When you are working with a chocolate mass it is good to have a few things going at once. The mass can overheat when you are working on it and therefore you might need to set aside half finished flowers or leafs if that is the case. If the mass overheats it will become very soft, greasy and difficult to work with.

• If the chocolate becomes greasy due to overheating it is good to lay it on a sponge and let it even out. This will make the shine go away. It is not recommended to use powdered food colors on the mass while it is greasy since the colors will smudge.

• Chocolate mass combines the advantages of fondant and marzipan. It has the white color and light texture of the fondant but it has a longer shelf life than marzipan and fondant. It is easily warmed up by hand and therefore it can be kept in the fridge and used long after it has been formed. By warming it a little bit, the decorations can be bent at will. The chocolate mass is usually used for thicker decorations. It can be used for thin decorations but working on it can be tricky and the room temperature needs to be quite low for it to work.

VANELLOPE'S RACE CAR BROWNIES

INGREDIENTS

- 1 (13 IN BY 9 IN) PAN PREPARED BROWNIES
- GRAHAM CRACKERS (OPTIONAL)
- 1 (2 LB) BAG CONFECTIONER'S SUGAR
- ½ C WATER
- 6 TBSP MERINGUE POWDER
- 32 PRETZELS STICKS
- 32 ROUND GOLDEN SANDWICH COOKIES
- 32 MINI CHOCOLATE SANDWICH COOKIES
- TUBES OF PREMADE ICING IN ASSORTED COLORS
- CANDY-COATED CHOCOLATE DROPS
- GUMDROPS
- GUMMY WORMS

TOOLS:

- PASTRY BAG OR GALLON-SIZED RESEALABLE BAG
- SCISSORS
- DECORATING ICING TIPS

In order to compete in the *Sugar Rush* races, Vanellope von Schweetz needs a speedy, candy-coated kart to drive. These candy-coated Race Car Brownies double as a party activity. Once you assemble the basic structure, kids can get creative and decorate their race cars with colorful icing and their favorite sweet treats.

INSTRUCTIONS

STEP 1 Prepare your favorite brownie recipe in a 13-inch-by-9-inch pan. Cool completely. Once brownies have cooled, cut with a sharp knife into four columns and four rows, for a total of sixteen brownies. (Note: a recipe that yields thick, cakey brownies is preferable. The brownies must be stiff enough to straddle their pretzel stick axels under the weight of icing and candy. In the event that your brownies turn out to be too gooey to hold their shape, they can be placed on a graham cracker chassis for support. A single 2½-by-1¼-inch graham cracker can be adhered to the underside of each brownie using the royal icing made in step 2. The axels would then be adhered to the surface of the graham cracker.)

STEP 2 In the bowl of an electric mixer, combine the confectioner's sugar, water, and meringue powder. Beat on medium speed for 7 minutes. Once royal icing has come together, transfer into a pastry bag fitted with a small round piping tip. If you don't have a pastry bag, you can use a gallon-sized resealable plastic bag. Use scissors to snip a tiny piece off one corner off the plastic bag.

STEP 3 To assemble each race car, you will need two pretzel sticks, two round golden sandwich cookies, two mini chocolate sandwich cookies, and the royal icing. First, flip the brownie over and pipe a thick line across the narrow dimension of the brownie, about ½ inch from one end. Repeat at the other end. Gently press a pretzel rod into each line of royal icing. These are the car's axels.

STEP 4 Pipe a generous amount of royal icing onto one side of each round golden sandwich cookie and press onto the sides of the brownie, one on each end of a pretzel stick. These are the rear wheels of the car. Then pipe royal icing onto one side of each mini

chocolate sandwich cookie and press onto the sides of the brownie, one on each end of the other pretzel stick. These are the front wheels of the race car.

STEP 5 Repeat steps 3 and 4 with the remaining brownies. Let sit for at least an hour while the royal icing sets and hardens.

STEP 6 When your little racers are ready to start their dessert engines, give each child a brownie race car. Provide an assortment of icing tubes fitted with various tips and candies for decorating. Candy-coated chocolate drops, gumdrops, and gummy worms work very well, but let your imagination run wild!

PLANES
PARTY

Planes (2013) takes to the skies, spinning the tale of a crop duster named Dusty Crophopper who has aspirations to become a racer. Supported by his friend Chug, mechanic Dottie, and coach Skipper, Dusty competes in an around-the-world air race. The course—and his fellow fliers—are challenging, but in the end, Dusty proves that your heart—not the way you're built—leads you to victory.

To prepare your child's Planes party for takeoff, first send out Dottie's Forklift Invitations. Once the racers have gathered on the runway, engage them in making Dusty Whirligigs, and then let them soar with Planes Racers. Little planes will definitely need to stop for fuel, so energize them with Dusty Nonstop Smoothies, Skipper Riley's Checkered Tail Fin Sandwich Tray, and Dusty Crophopper Cupcakes. Before they taxi back to their hangars, send each racer home with a Candy Plane Favor.

DOTTIE'S FORKLIFT INVITATIONS

MAKES 2 INVITATIONS

Working as a mechanic in Propwash Junction, Dottie has surely fixed her fair share of turbines. Pragmatic and caring, she isn't shy about warning Dusty of the dangers of racing. But when she sees how desperately he wants to win, she supports him unflinchingly. Complete with silver forklifts, these invites are a great way to get your *Planes* party off the ground.

MATERIALS

- ❤ DOTTIE'S FORKLIFT INVITATIONS TEMPLATE (P. 169)
- ❤ 1 (9 IN BY 12 IN) SHEET LIGHT BLUE HEAVYWEIGHT CRAFT PAPER OR (8½ IN BY 11 IN) CARD STOCK
- ❤ 1 (9 IN BY 12 IN) SHEET BLACK HEAVYWEIGHT CRAFT PAPER OR (8½ IN BY 11 IN) CARD STOCK
- ❤ 1 (9 IN BY 12 IN) SHEET WHITE HEAVYWEIGHT CRAFT PAPER OR (8½ IN BY 11 IN) CARD STOCK
- ❤ 1 (9 IN BY 12 IN) SHEET SILVER OR GRAY HEAVYWEIGHT CRAFT PAPER OR (8½ IN BY 11 IN) CARD STOCK
- ❤ 1 (9 IN BY 12 IN) SHEET BROWN HEAVYWEIGHT CRAFT PAPER OR (8½ IN BY 11 IN) CARD STOCK
- ❤ WHITE CRAFT PAINT
- ❤ 4 (⅜ IN) SILVER SEQUINS
- ❤ 4 (¼ IN) RED FAUX GEMS
- ❤ ENVELOPES (OPTIONAL)

TOOLS:
- ❤ SCISSORS
- ❤ PENCIL
- ❤ GLUE STICK
- ❤ TOOTHPICK
- ❤ FINE-TIP BLACK PERMANENT MARKER

NOTE → The materials can be scaled up for the number of guests invited to your party.

INSTRUCTIONS

STEP 1 Using the Dottie's Forklift Invitations template on page 169, make a photocopy enlarging it 200 percent. Carefully cut out all of the shapes—this will be your master template.

STEP 2 Trace the forklift body and the upper and lower windshield trim pieces onto a sheet of light blue heavyweight craft paper or card stock. Cut out the pieces.

STEP 3 Trace the windshield backing, two tires, and two pupils onto a sheet of black heavyweight craft paper or card stock. Cut out the pieces.

STEP 4 Trace the windshield onto a sheet of white heavyweight craft paper or card stock and cut it out.

STEP 5 Trace two grills, two forks, and two wheel covers onto a sheet of silver or gray heavyweight craft paper or card stock. Cut out the pieces.

STEP 6 Trace two irises onto a sheet of brown heavyweight craft paper or card stock and cut them out.

STEP 7 Begin by assembling the windshield. Apply glue to the back of the light blue upper windshield trim piece and adhere it to the black windshield backing piece, positioned at the top, leaving about ⅛ inch of the black backing showing at the top edge.

STEP 8 Apply glue to the back of the white windshield piece and adhere it to the black windshield backing piece, positioning it so that about ⅛ inch of the black backing is visible between the light blue upper windshield trim and the white windshield.

STEP 9 Apply glue to the back of the light blue lower windshield trim piece and adhere it to the black windshield backing piece, positioning it so that about inch of the black backing shows along the bottom edge.

STEP 10 To assemble the eyes, apply glue to the backs of the black pupils and adhere them to the brown iris pieces, positioning them very slightly above and to the right of center. Glue them to the white windshield, using the circles on the template as reference for positioning. Use the tip of a toothpick to apply a tiny spot of white paint to the upper right edge of each pupil. Set the windshield aside and wait for the paint to dry.

STEP 11 While the windshield is drying, apply glue to the backs of the black tires and adhere one on each side of the light blue forklift body so the edges are flush. Apply glue to the backs of the silver/gray wheel covers and adhere them to the tops of the tires so the edges are flush.

STEP 12 To assemble the grill and forks, place the two grill pieces on your work surface so that their long dimensions are parallel and facing you, spaced about ⅜ inch apart. Fold each of the fork pieces in half. With the pieces still folded, apply glue to the back of each fork (so if they were unfolded, the top half of one side would have glue on it). Adhere the forks atop the two grill pieces so that they are perpendicular to the grills, the folds are positioned at the bottom of the grill so the forks will open toward you, and the outside edges of the forks are flush with the outside edges of the grills.

STEP 13 Apply glue to the back of the grill-and-forks piece and adhere it atop the forklift body, positioned between—and slightly overlapping—the two tires.

STEP 14 Glue the finished windshield in place, using the outline on the forklift body piece as reference for placement.

STEP 15 To make Dottie's smile, cut a thin crescent-moon shape about 1½ inches wide from a sheet of black paper and glue it to the forklift body about ¾ inch below the windshield. (Or you can draw it on: use a pencil first to sketch it in lightly, and once you're satisfied with the positioning, go over it with a fine point black permanent marker.)

STEP 16 Glue a silver sequin to each of the wheel covers, positioning them so they extend slightly above the top edge of each wheel cover. Adhere a red faux gem to the center of each sequin.

STEP 17 To make the information card that will sit in Dottie's forks, cut a 3¼-by-2¼-inch rectangle from the white heavyweight craft paper or card stock, and write "You're invited to a Planes party!" on the front. Then write the party particulars on the back. Place the card on Dottie's forks, fold the bottom halves of the forks up over the card, and slip the invite into an envelope.

DUSTY WHIRLIGIGS

MAKES 1 FAVOR

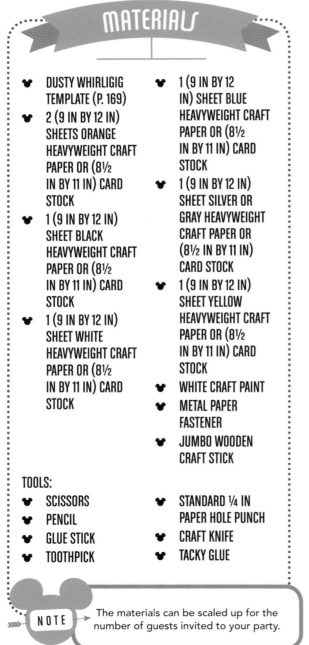

MATERIALS

- DUSTY WHIRLIG TEMPLATE (P. 169)
- 2 (9 IN BY 12 IN) SHEETS ORANGE HEAVYWEIGHT CRAFT PAPER OR (8½ IN BY 11 IN) CARD STOCK
- 1 (9 IN BY 12 IN) SHEET BLACK HEAVYWEIGHT CRAFT PAPER OR (8½ IN BY 11 IN) CARD STOCK
- 1 (9 IN BY 12 IN) SHEET WHITE HEAVYWEIGHT CRAFT PAPER OR (8½ IN BY 11 IN) CARD STOCK
- 1 (9 IN BY 12 IN) SHEET BLUE HEAVYWEIGHT CRAFT PAPER OR (8½ IN BY 11 IN) CARD STOCK
- 1 (9 IN BY 12 IN) SHEET SILVER OR GRAY HEAVYWEIGHT CRAFT PAPER OR (8½ IN BY 11 IN) CARD STOCK
- 1 (9 IN BY 12 IN) SHEET YELLOW HEAVYWEIGHT CRAFT PAPER OR (8½ IN BY 11 IN) CARD STOCK
- WHITE CRAFT PAINT
- METAL PAPER FASTENER
- JUMBO WOODEN CRAFT STICK

TOOLS:
- SCISSORS
- PENCIL
- GLUE STICK
- TOOTHPICK
- STANDARD ¼ IN PAPER HOLE PUNCH
- CRAFT KNIFE
- TACKY GLUE

NOTE The materials can be scaled up for the number of guests invited to your party.

Dusty might come from a small town, but he has big dreams: he hopes to become a world-class racer. Despite his fear of heights, his functional build, and the naysayers who doubt him, he never loses sight of the finish line. Building these whirligig favors is a great party activity for little *Planes* fans. The pieces can be cut out in advance, and then kids can assemble them as part of the festivities.

INSTRUCTIONS

STEP 1 Using the Dusty's Whirligig template on page 169, make a photocopy enlarging it 200 percent. Carefully cut out all of the shapes—this will be your master template.

STEP 2 Trace two plane frames (one for the front and one for the back), the windshield top trim piece, and the windshield bottom trim piece onto a sheet of orange heavyweight craft paper or card stock. Cut out the pieces.

STEP 3 Trace the windshield backing, mouth, propeller, and two pupils onto a sheet of black heavyweight craft paper or card stock. Cut out the pieces.

STEP 4 Trace the plane nose and the windshield onto a sheet of white heavyweight craft paper or card stock and cut them out.

STEP 5 Trace two irises onto a sheet of blue heavyweight craft paper or card stock and cut them out.

STEP 6 Trace the propeller nose onto a sheet of silver or gray heavyweight craft paper or card stock and cut it out.

STEP 7   Trace three propeller tips onto a sheet of yellow heavyweight craft paper or card stock and cut them out.

STEP 8   Begin by assembling the windshield. First, apply glue to the back of the white windshield piece and adhere it to the black windshield backing piece, positioning it so that a narrow black border is visible around the entire perimeter. Apply glue to the back of the orange windshield top trim piece and adhere it to white windshield so that the top edges are flush (narrow black border should still be visible). Apply glue to the back of the orange windshield bottom trim piece and adhere it to white windshield so that the bottom edges are flush (again, narrow black border should still be visible).

STEP 9   To make Dusty's eyes, apply glue to the backs of the black pupils and adhere one centered on each of the blue irises. Apply glue to the backs of the assembled eyes and adhere to the center of the exposed white windshield, positioning them about 3/8 inch apart from each other. Use the tip of a toothpick to apply a tiny spot of white paint to the upper right edge of each pupil. Set the windshield aside and wait for the paint to dry.

STEP 10   While the windshield is drying, apply glue to the backs of the three yellow propeller tips and adhere one to the end of each black propeller blade, positioning them so that the edges are flush. Apply glue to the back of the silver or gray propeller nose piece, and adhere it in the center of the black propeller piece. Use the hole punch to punch a hole in the center of the assembled propeller nose.

STEP 11   Apply glue to the back of the white plane nose piece and adhere it to one of the orange plane frame pieces. Use a craft knife to cut a small slit through the middle of the plane nose just large enough so that the prongs of the paper fastener will fit through later.

STEP 12   Insert the prongs of the paper fastener through the hole you punched in the propeller nose so that the head of the fastener is on the side with the gray or silver propeller nose and yellow propeller tips. Now insert the prongs into the slit you cut in the plane nose. On the back of the orange plane frame, fold out the prongs of the fastener, making sure that the fit allows enough room for the propeller to spin freely.

STEP 13   Apply glue to the back of the assembled windshield piece and adhere atop the orange plane frame, positioning it ½ inch from the top of the frame. Apply glue to the back of the black mouth piece and adhere to the orange plane frame, positioning it ¼ inch below the windshield.

STEP 14   Apply tacky glue to the top third of the wooden craft stick. Adhere it, centered, to the second orange plane frame piece. Apply more glue to the orange plane frame on either side and above the craft stick, although be sure to avoid the area where the prongs of the paper fastener will be situated. Place the assembled front plane frame atop the back frame, sandwiching the craft stick between them, and making sure edges are flush. Press firmly to ensure a strong bond and let glue dry before use.

PLANES RACERS

MAKES 3 RACERS

If there's one thing that Dusty Crophopper proves by winning the Wings Around the Globe rally, it's that heart is more important than a fancy propeller or a turbo-charged engine. Made with craft foam, paper clips, and rubber bands, these *Planes* Racers definitely don't have fancy propellers or turbo-charged engines, but with the help of some enthusiastic party guests, they can fly nonstop across the living room!

MATERIALS

- *PLANES* RACERS TEMPLATE (P. 168)
- 1 (9 IN BY 12 IN) SHEET ORANGE CRAFT FOAM
- 1 (8½ IN BY 11 IN) SHEET WHITE CARD STOCK
- 3 SMALL PAPER CLIPS
- 3 (3 IN LONG) THIN RUBBER BANDS

TOOLS:
- SCISSORS
- PENCIL
- CRAFT KNIFE
- FINE POINT BLACK PERMANENT MARKER
- TOOTHPICK
- TACKY GLUE

NOTE The materials can be scaled up for the number of guests invited to your party.

INSTRUCTIONS

STEP 1 Using the *Planes* Racers template on page 168, make a photocopy enlarging it 200 percent. Carefully cut out all of the shapes—this will be your master template

STEP 2 For each racer, trace and cut one body, one tail fin, and one wings piece from a sheet of orange craft foam. Trace and cut two front windows and two side windows from a piece of white card stock.

STEP 3 With the template as a guide for all your cuts, use the craft knife to cut the slit in the body of the plane. Use scissors to cut the slit in the tail end of the plane body, the slit in the tail fin, and the two slits in the wings piece.

STEP 4 To create each racer's eyes, use the black marker to draw a half circle flush against the middle of the left edge of one of the white front windows. This will be the left eye. Flip over the second white front window and draw a half circle flush against the middle of the right

edge. This will be the right eye.

STEP 5 Dip the toothpick in the tacky glue and apply glue to the back of the left eye. Adhere it to the left side of the plane body so that the front edge of the window is flush with the front edge of the craft foam. Flip the plane body over and repeat with the right eye on the right side.

STEP 6 Flip over one of the side windows. One should now have its straight edge facing left (the left side window) and the other should have its straight edge facing right (the right side window). Apply tacky glue to the back of the left side window and adhere atop the plane body, about ⅛ in to the right of the left eye. Flip the plane body over and repeat with the right side window on the right side of the

plane body. Allow the glue to dry completely.

STEP 7 Fold the wings piece in half along the center line of its long dimension and insert through the slit in the plane body. Unfold the wings piece and adjust the position so the slits in the wings piece grip the body of the plane.

STEP 8 Use the rubber band to tie a cow-hitch knot at one end of the paper clip. Slide the other end of the paper clip onto the nose of the plane body. To make the plane fly, loop the free end of the rubber band over your left thumb and hold your left hand steady. Grip the underside of the plane nose (including the paper clip) with your right hand and pull it back to stretch the rubber band. Aim, let go of the rubber band, and watch it soar!

MAKES 8 CANDY FAVORS

MATERIALS

- BLUE CRAFT PAPER IN A VARIETY OF PATTERNS
- ORANGE CRAFT PAPER IN A VARIETY OF PATTERNS
- 8 STICKS OF GUM, IN WRAPPERS
- 8 ROLLS OF SMARTIES™ CANDIES, IN WRAPPERS
- 8 (3 IN LONG) THIN RUBBER BANDS
- 16 LIFESAVERS™ MINT CANDIES, WHITE, UNWRAPPED

TOOLS:

- PENCIL
- RULER
- SCISSORS
- GLUE STICK

 NOTE → The materials can be scaled up for the number of guests invited to your party.

Dusty Crophopper knows that there is nothing sweeter than victory, especially when most of the world thought you wouldn't succeed. If you're looking for a hint of sweet victory to dole out to your party guests, these *Planes* Candy Favors are just the ticket. Comprised of Smarties™, LifeSavers™, and sticks of gum, these tiny treats are decked out in the *Planes* colors and make a satisfying finish to a high-flying party.

INSTRUCTIONS

STEP 1   For each favor, measure and cut a 2½-by-2¾-inch rectangle of either blue or orange craft paper. Wrap the rectangle around a stick of gum and use the glue stick to apply adhesive to the overlapping edge of the paper, adhering it to the edge underneath it.

STEP 2   Measure and cut a 2-inch square from a different color and/or pattern of craft paper. Wrap it around a roll of Smarties™ and secure using the glue stick.

STEP 3   To assemble the favor, thread both ends of the rubber band through the holes in two LifeSavers™. Set the roll of Smarties™ on the rubber band "hammock" between the two LifeSavers™. Place the stick of gum atop the roll of Smarties™, above the LifeSaver™ wheels, perpendicular to the roll of Smarties™. Pull up the ends of the rubber band and slip over the tip of the stick of gum on the corresponding side.

DUSTY NONSTOP SMOOTHIES

MATERIALS

- DUSTY NONSTOP SMOOTHIE PROPELLER TEMPLATE (P. 169)
- 1 (9 IN BY 12 IN) SHEET BLUE CRAFT FOAM
- 8 PAPER HOLE REINFORCEMENT STICKERS
- 8 FLEXIBLE ORANGE DRINKING STRAWS

INGREDIENTS:

- 2 C ORANGE JUICE
- 1 LARGE BANANA
- 2 C FROZEN MANGO CUBES
- VANILLA FROZEN YOGURT (OR WHIPPED CREAM)

TOOLS:

- SCISSORS
- PENCIL
- CRAFT KNIFE

When you're flying nonstop across the Pacific Ocean, you need high-octane fuel to keep you going. Dusty would never fill his tank with anything but the best, and neither should little partygoers. That's why these smoothies are fantastic party food: they're made from nutrient-packed bananas, mangos, orange juice, and frozen yogurt, and they taste heavenly!

INSTRUCTIONS

STEP 1 Using the Dusty Nonstop Smoothie propeller template on page 169, make a photocopy, enlarging it 200 percent. Carefully cut out the shape—this will be your master template.

STEP 2 Trace the template eight times onto the sheet of blue craft foam and cut out the propellers.

STEP 3 Use the craft knife to cut a small X in the center of each propeller. Adhere a paper hole reinforcement sticker to the center of the propeller so it encircles the X-shaped cut. Push the bottom tip of a straw through the X-shaped cut in each propeller, and slide the propeller up to the top bendable portion.

STEP 4 To make the smoothies, combine the orange juice, banana, and frozen mango cubes in a blender. Puree until the mixture is thick and creamy. Divide the mixture among eight glasses and top each glass with a small "cloud" of vanilla frozen yogurt (or whipped cream). Insert a propeller straw in each glass and serve immediately.

SKIPPER RILEY'S CHECKERED TAIL FIN SANDWICH TRAY

MAKES 24 (1½ IN) SQUARE SANDWICHES

MATERIALS

- 6 SLICES WHITE SANDWICH BREAD
- 4 TO 6 SLICES PUMPERNICKEL BREAD (OR DARK WHEAT, IF YOU PREFER)
- ½ LB SLICED TURKEY OR OTHER DELI MEAT
- 1 (8 OZ) CONTAINER OF WHIPPED CREAM CHEESE

TOOLS:

- BREAD KNIFE
- RULER
- PASTRY BAG WITH ⅜ IN OR ½ IN TIP

Legendary war hero Skipper Riley is hesitant when Dusty first asks for some coaching. But he later proves to be a valuable and courageous ally, helping Dusty hone his racing skills and fighting off malicious maneuvers from Ripslinger. Echoing the flight instructor's checkered tail fin, this sandwich tray is made with squares of pumpernickel and white bread—and it also happens to resemble a victory flag!

INSTRUCTIONS

STEP 1 Using a bread knife, cut the crusts off all the slices of bread. Cut twenty-four squares, 1½ inches wide, from the slices of white bread. Cut an additional twenty-four squares, 1½ inches wide, from the slices of pumpernickel bread. Set aside.

STEP 2 Cut twenty-four squares, 1 inch wide, from the slices of turkey (or other deli meat).

STEP 3 Transfer whipped cream cheese into a pastry bag fitted with a ⅜-inch or ½-inch round tip. Pipe a small amount of cream cheese onto each of the pumpernickel squares.

STEP 4 Place a turkey square atop the cream cheese on each pumpernickel square so that the meat is centered on the bread and the cut edges are parallel. Press down gently.

STEP 5 Pipe a small amount of cream cheese atop each of the turkey squares. Place a square of white bread atop the cream cheese on each turkey square so the edges of the pumpernickel square and the white bread square are flush. Press down gently to adhere the bread and filling.

STEP 6 Flip half of the sandwiches over so the pumpernickel side is face-up. Arrange the sandwiches on a tray in six rows of four, alternating white-side-up and pumpernickel-side-up so the presentation resembles a checkerboard. Refrigerate until ready to serve.

DUSTY CROPHOPPER CUPCAKES

MAKES 12 CUPCAKES

MATERIALS

- DUSTY CROPHOPPER CUPCAKES TEMPLATE (P. 168)
- TRACING PAPER (OPTIONAL)
- 1 (9 IN BY 12 IN) SHEET BLACK HEAVYWEIGHT CRAFT PAPER
- 1 (9 IN BY 12 IN) SHEET YELLOW HEAVYWEIGHT CRAFT PAPER
- 1 (9 IN BY 12 IN) SHEET SILVER HEAVYWEIGHT CRAFT PAPER

INGREDIENTS:

- 6 (2¼ IN BY 5 IN) WHOLE GRAHAM CRACKER SHEETS
- 1 (7 OZ) PACKAGE WHITE COOKIE ICING
- ORANGE FOOD COLORING
- PALM-SIZE BALL OF BLACK FONDANT
- 24 BLUE CANDY BEADS FROM CANDY NECKLACES
- 13 TOOTHPICKS
- POWDERED SUGAR, FOR ROLLING
- FAVORITE RECIPE FOR 1 DOZEN CUPCAKES, PREPARED IN ORANGE OR WHITE CUPCAKE LINERS, ICED WITH ORANGE FROSTING
- 12 LIFESAVERS MINT CANDIES, WHITE, UNWRAPPED

TOOLS:

- KITCHEN KNIFE
- PENCIL
- SCISSORS
- WAX PAPER
- ROLLING PIN
- PLASTIC WRAP
- GLUE STICK
- PUSHPIN

NOTE → It is best to make the windshields and propellers the day before making the cupcakes.

Dusty Crophopper is a plane of many talents: he excels at dusting crops, flies past the competition in the Wings Around the Globe rally, and comes to the rescue putting out forest fires in *Planes: Fire and Rescue*. Pay homage to this brave little flier by making Dusty Crophopper cupcakes, topped with graham-cracker windshields and paper propellers. This dessert is sure to finish off any *Planes* party with flying colors.

INSTRUCTIONS

STEP 1   Carefully break each graham cracker sheet in half, along the short center line, resulting in a dozen 2½-by-2¼-inch rectangles. These will be the windshields that sit atop the cupcakes. Place a graham cracker on your work surface so one of the shorter (2¼-inch) sides is closest to you. Use a kitchen knife to carefully cut each side at a diagonal, creating a trapezoid that is 1½ inches wide at the top and 2 inches wide at the bottom. Repeat with remaining graham crackers. Frost the windshields with white cookie icing, covering one face completely, all the way to the edges. Set aside to harden.

STEP 2   Of the remaining white cookie icing, reserve 1 tablespoon and set aside. Place the rest in a small bowl and add orange food coloring. Stir until color is uniform and desired shade of orange is achieved. Cover and set aside.

STEP 3   To create the eyes, pinch a tiny bit of black fondant from the ball and roll into an oblong pellet shape, insert one end of the pellet into the hole in the center of a blue candy necklace bead, and gently press down on the fondant to create a circular pupil in the center of the blue iris. Repeat with remaining blue candy necklace beads.

STEP 4   If desired, use a toothpick to gently poke a tiny hole in the upper right edge of each pupil, and then fill with a dot of white icing to create a glint. Reserve the remaining white icing.

STEP 5 Once the frosted windshields have hardened, use the orange icing to frost bands across the upper and lower portions of the windshields, leaving a white band across the center about ¾ inch tall.

STEP 6 Use the toothpick to apply a bit of the reserved white icing to the back of each assembled eye. Position two eyes on the center line of the white band of each windshield, about ¼ inch apart, in the middle. Set windshields aside to harden.

STEP 7 Using the Dusty Crophopper Cupcake template on page 168, make a photocopy enlarging it 200 percent. Carefully cut out the shapes.

STEP 8 Cover the work surface with a sheet of wax paper and sprinkle with powdered sugar. Roll out the remainder of the black fondant ball to a 3/8-inch thickness, dusting the fondant and rolling pin with additional powdered sugar if it begins to stick. Place the mouth template piece on top of the rolled-out fondant and use a sharp kitchen knife to trace around the outside edge. Repeat eleven more times and cover mouth pieces with plastic wrap.

STEP 9 To make the propellers for the cupcakes, trace the propeller template piece onto a sheet of black heavyweight craft paper, tracing twelve propellers (one per cupcake). Cut out and set aside.

STEP 10 Trace the propeller tip template piece onto a sheet of yellow heavyweight craft paper, tracing thirty-six propeller tips (three per cupcake). Cut out and set aside.

STEP 11 Trace the propeller center template piece onto a sheet of silver heavyweight craft paper, tracing twelve propellers (one per cupcake). Cut out and set aside.

STEP 12 Use the glue stick to adhere the yellow propeller tips to the ends of the propeller blades, positioning them so the curved edges are flush.

STEP 13 Use the pushpin to poke a hole through the center of the black circular hub of each propeller. Insert the tip of a toothpick through the hole in each propeller

hub. Gently bend a small portion of the tip of each toothpick, making sure not to break it off completely, so the propeller won't slide off the toothpick.

STEP 14 Glue each silver propeller center atop the circular black propeller hub, sandwiching the bent portion of the toothpick in between the silver and black paper.

STEP 15 In orange or white cupcake liners, prepare your favorite recipe for one dozen cupcakes. Once cupcakes are completely cool, frost with orange icing. Use a knife to make a narrow cut across the center of each cupcake, and then insert the bottom of an assembled windshield into the cut, pushing it in just enough so that it will stand up.

STEP 16 Place a white LifeSaver candy atop the icing on the front edge of each cupcake, abutting the paper liner. Insert the toothpick end of a propeller into the hole in each LifeSaver, pushing down into the cupcake so the propeller hub sits on top of the LifeSaver.

STEP 17 Finally, place the black fondant mouth pieces atop the iced cupcakes, just below the windshields, with the curved edges closest to the windshields. Keep in a cool, dry place until ready to serve.

WHO'S THE BOSS?

······················· GAME FOR 10–25 GUESTS ·······················

Dusty knows it's important to give the right instructions at the right time. But it's not easy if you have to do it in secret ... and with someone trying to find out who's the boss!

INSTRUCTIONS

STEP 1 Gather the guests in a tight circle. The group decides who is to be the Guesser, who is then escorted out of the room.

STEP 2 Then the group decides who is to be The Boss.

STEP 3 The Guesser is brought back in and placed in the middle of the circle.

STEP 4 The Boss decides in secret what the whole group does. If he wants to clap hands then he starts clapping his hands. The group has to follow his lead as fast as possible.

STEP 5 The Guesser has to find out who The Boss is. *How* The Boss secretly indicates to the group what to do is the catch. If The Guesser manages to expose The Boss he is then out of the game.

CAPTAIN HOOK
PARTY

One of the most dastardly villains to ever sail the seven seas, Captain Hook made his debut onstage in J. M. Barrie's 1904 play *Peter Pan; or, the Boy Who Wouldn't Grow Up.* Since then, the pirate has appeared in novels, television shows, and films—most notably, Disney's animated feature *Peter Pan* (1953). Having lost his left hand in a duel with Peter, Hook keeps the *Jolly Roger* anchored in Never Land, intent on exacting his revenge.

To alert little scalawags of an impending piratical celebration, start by sending out Captain Hook's Hook Invitations. On the day of the briny bash, decorate with the Tick-Tock Crocodile Garland, then engage mini-marauders with the Trivia Treasure Hunt. In the galley, whip up some Tricorn Hat Bean and Cheese Pockets, Skull Rock Watermelon Fruit Salad, and the *Jolly Roger* Pirate Ship Cake, and your rapscallion crew is sure to be sated. Don't forget to send the seafarers home with some booty: Pirate Flag Pennants will please seasoned seadogs and landlubbers alike!

CAPTAIN HOOK'S HOOK INVITATIONS

MAKES 4 INVITATIONS

MATERIALS

- CAPTAIN HOOK INVITATION TEMPLATE (P. 167)
- 1 (12 IN SQUARE) SHEET TEAL-BLUE CARD STOCK
- 1 (12 IN SQUARE) SHEET RED CARD STOCK
- 1 (12 IN SQUARE) SHEET WHITE CARD STOCK
- 1 (12 IN SQUARE) SHEET SILVER CARD STOCK

TOOLS:
- SCISSORS
- PENCIL
- RULER
- GLUE STICK
- ULTRA FINE POINT BLACK PERMANENT MARKER

NOTE The materials can be scaled up for the number of guests invited to your party.

Named for the iron appendage that replaced his left hand after he lost it during a duel with Peter Pan, Captain Hook is a fearsome and volatile pirate. While the privateer's true name is something of a mystery, his pirate name is synonymous with ruthlessness, determination, and style. And since nothing says "Captain Hook" like the hook itself, these card stock invitations are the perfect way to proclaim a pirate party.

INSTRUCTIONS

STEP 1 Using the Captain Hook Invitation template on page 167, make a photocopy enlarging it 200 percent. Carefully cut out all of the shapes—this will be your master template.

STEP 2 For each invitation, cut a 7-by-4-inch rectangle from the teal-blue card stock.

STEP 3 Trace the sleeve cuff onto a sheet of red card stock and cut it out.

STEP 4 Trace the lace trim onto a sheet of white card stock and cut it out.

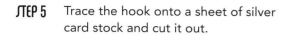

STEP 5 Trace the hook onto a sheet of silver card stock and cut it out.

STEP 6 Use the glue stick to apply adhesive to the back of the red sleeve cuff. Adhere it atop the teal-blue rectangle, positioning the sleeve cuff so it is centered within the narrow dimension of the rectangle, with the wider end of the cuff about ¼ inch from one of the narrow ends of the teal-blue rectangle.

STEP 7 Apply glue to the back of the lace trim and adhere it atop the blue rectangle so the curve of the trim is flush with the curve at the top of the sleeve cuff. Do not press down the center of the top edge; the hook will need to slide underneath it.

STEP 8 Apply glue to the back of the silver hook and adhere atop the teal-blue rectangle so the base of the hook is centered within the lace trim and the top edge of the hook is just shy of the top edge of the teal-blue rectangle. Tuck the tip of the base of the hook under the white lace trim and press both pieces firmly. Set aside to let glue dry.

STEP 9 Use a ultra fine point black permanent marker to write, "You're Invited to a Captain Hook Party!" in the red sleeve cuff area. Turn the invite over and write the party details on the back.

TICK-TOCK CROCODILE GARLAND

MAKES 1 (96-IN) GARLAND

MATERIALS

- TICK-TOCK CROCODILE GARLAND TEMPLATE (P. 167)
- 2 (12 IN SQUARE) SHEETS EMERALD-GREEN CARD STOCK (MAKES 6 CROCS)
- 1 (12 IN SQUARE) SHEET LIME-GREEN CARD STOCK (MAKES 8 CROCS)
- 12 (7 MM) GOOGLY EYES
- 1 (8 FT) LENGTH RIBBON IN YOUR COLOR OF CHOICE, ½ IN WIDE

TOOLS:

- SCISSORS
- PENCIL
- GLUE STICK
- HOT GLUE GUN

NOTE → The materials can be scaled up for the number of guests invited to your party.

The only sound that Captain Hook fears is the tick-tock that emits from the belly of the crocodile that doggedly pursues him. Ever since Peter Pan cut off Hook's hand and threw it to the crocodile, the reptile has been hungry for the rest of the pirate captain. Made out of green card stock and embellished with googly eyes, these crocs can be strung on a ribbon and hung around the party room or draped across the front of the buffet table.

INSTRUCTIONS

STEP 1 Using the Tick-Tock Crocodile Garland template on page 167, make a photocopy enlarging it 200 percent. Carefully cut out all of the shapes—this will be your master template.

STEP 2 Trace six croc bodies onto the sheets of emerald-green card stock. Cut out and set aside.

STEP 3 Trace six bellies and six chests onto a sheet of lime-green card stock. Cut out the pieces.

STEP 4 Use the glue stick to apply adhesive to the back of the belly piece. Adhere on top of the croc body so that the bottom edges of the belly are flush. Apply glue to the back of the chest piece and adhere on top of the croc body so that the leftmost edges of the croc's chest are flush.

STEP 5 Apply a tiny dab of hot glue to the back of a googly eye. Position about ⅛ inch from the top of a croc's head, to the left of center. Apply a tiny dab of hot glue to the back of a second googly eye. Position about ⅛ inch from the top of the croc's head, to the right of center. Repeat with the remaining crocs.

STEP 6 To string the crocs together, measure a length of ½-inch ribbon about 8 feet long. Beginning about 2 feet from one end of the ribbon, apply a line of hot glue along the center of the ribbon about 4 inches long. Set a croc on top of the glue, positioning the ribbon just under the ridge of his back. Leaving a gap of a couple inches behind the first croc's tail, apply another 4-inch line of hot glue and adhere another croc. Repeat with remaining crocs. To display, tape or tack the free ends of the ribbon to a doorway, a wall, or a buffet table.

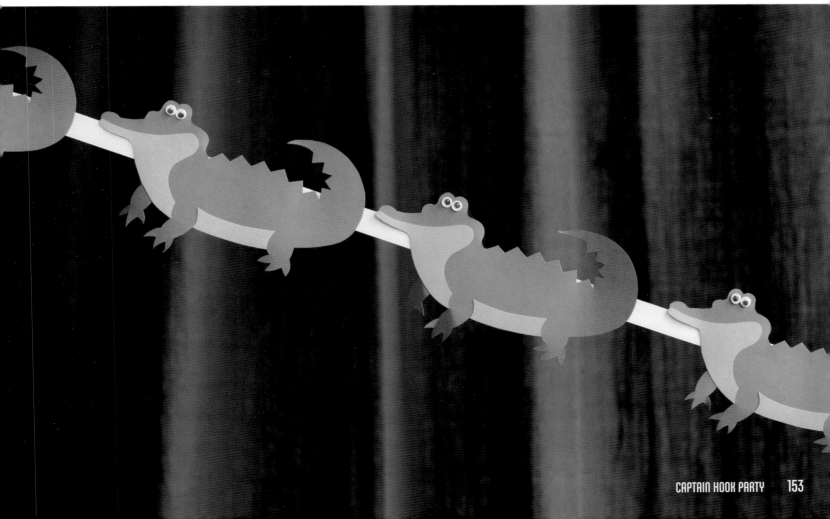

TRIVIA TREASURE HUNT

MAKES 1 SET OF 10 TRIVIA CARDS AND 1 TREASURE CHEST

MATERIALS

- 10 (3 IN BY 5 IN) INDEX CARDS
- 1 (6 IN) UNFINISHED WOODEN TREASURE CHEST*
- YELLOW ACRYLIC PAINT
- BROWN ACRYLIC PAINT
- CHOCOLATE GOLD COINS
- BRIGHTLY COLORED (JEWELRY-SHAPED) HARD CANDIES
- CANDY NECKLACES
- SCRAP PAPER
- PENCILS

TOOLS:

- BLACK PERMANENT MARKER
- SMALL PAINTBRUSH
- MEDIUM PAINTBRUSH

NOTE The materials can be scaled up for the number of guests invited to your party.

*Unfinished wooden boxes are carried at most large craft stores.

No spyglass, map, or compass is needed to find this bountiful treasure—just a thorough knowledge of Captain Hook. Copy the provided trivia questions onto index cards and then prepare the booty: a painted wooden treasure chest that you can fill with chocolate gold coins and other goodies. Whichever team or individual answers the most questions correctly gets to take home the plunder!

INSTRUCTIONS

STEP 1   Use a permanent marker to copy the following questions onto index cards. Write "Trivia Treasure Hunt" on one side of each card, and write a question with its four possible answers on the other side. (The correct answers are underlined.)

1. Captain Hook's ship is anchored in:
   a) <u>Cannibal Cove</u>
   b) Mermaid Lagoon
   c) Buccaneer Bay
   d) Privateer Harbor

2. Hook can tell when the crocodile is nearby because the croc swallowed:
   a) A cow bell
   b) A fog horn
   c) <u>An alarm clock</u>
   d) A cell phone

3. When Mr. Smee intends to shave Captain Hook's face, he accidentally shaves:

   a) His own arms

   b) <u>A seagull's backside</u>

   c) Peter Pan's head

   d) Hook's legs

4. Thinking this person might know the location of Peter's hideout, Hook kidnaps:

   a) Wendy

   b) <u>Princess Tiger Lily</u>

   c) John

   d) Cubby

5. Peter Pan's nickname for Captain Hook is:

   a) Flounder

   b) Clownfish

   c) Marlin

   d) <u>Codfish</u>

6. Captain Hook's crew wants to go out to sea, but Hook keeps the ship in Never Land because:

   a) Hook hasn't found the treasure at Blind Man's Bluff

   b) <u>Hook wants revenge on Peter Pan</u>

   c) The ship has a hole in its hull

   d) The ship's sails need repairing

7. Hook tricks Tinker Bell into revealing the location of Peter's hideout by promising:

   a) To send Wendy home to London

   b) To make Wendy walk the plank

   c) <u>To take Wendy to sea with him</u>

   d) To maroon Wendy on Skull Rock

8. When trying to convince the Lost Boys and the Darlings to become pirates, Hook promises to give them:

   a) A free tattoo

   b) <u>A gold doubloon</u>

   c) An eye patch

   d) A bandana

9. The package that Hook lowers into Peter's hideout contains:

   a) A poisoned cake

   b) A scorpion

   c) A snake

   c) <u>A bomb</u>

10. Captain Hook's ship is called:

    a) Never Land Lady

    b) Pirate's Bounty

    a) <u>Jolly Roger</u>

    d) Tomfoolery

STEP 2 To create the treasure chest prize, begin by using a small paintbrush and yellow acrylic paint to add embellishments and "brass" trim to the bare wooden chest. Then use a medium-sized brush to paint the remaining area brown, including the inside of the chest. Let the chest dry completely.

STEP 3 Once the chest is dry, fill it with an assortment of chocolate golden coins, brightly colored hard candies, and candy necklaces.

HOW TO PLAY

When it's time to play, divide partygoers into teams or allow them to play individually. For younger players, the game can be made easier by omitting one of the incorrect answers for each question. Give each team a piece of scrap paper and a pencil with which to take down their answers (be sure they also write down their names). Read aloud each question followed by its possible answers, and instruct players to write down the question number followed by which-ever option—A, B, C, or D—they believe to be correct. Once all the questions have been read, collect the players' answer sheets and tally up the points. Whichever individual/team has earned the most points wins the treasure chest!

CANNONBALL!

GAME FOR 5 – 15 GUESTS

MATERIALS

- 1 THROWING BALL
- AN OPEN FIELD

Captain Hook's greatest enemies are Peter Pan and the Lost Boys. He is forever confounded by those pesky rascals! And what is worse is that they can fly! But Hook has a weapon that can shoot them out of the sky. His cannon!

INSTRUCTIONS

It's everybody for himself. One player begins the game by throwing up the cannonball shouting "Now you'll get it, you raskaly rats!"

Everyone tries to catch the cannonball. The one who succeds yells "Cannonball!" and everyone imediately freezes. Then he tries to shoot down the other frozen players. If he hits one, then that player is out of the game.

A player is not hit if the ball touches the ground before hitting him or if he is shot in the head. If a player grabs the ball in mid air (before it touches the ground) the thrower is out of the game.

A player can get back into the game when the person that hit him originally is out.

The game ends when one player is left. He is the winner and gets to throw the cannonball in the next game.

Abbreviations:

1. A player cannot be shot down if the thrower is so close that they can shake hands.
2. Someone's name can be shouted out when the cannonball is thrown. That person is then the only one who can catch the cannonball.

PIRATE FLAG PENNANT

MAKES 4 PENNANTS

MATERIALS

- PIRATE PENNANT TEMPLATE (P. 167)
- 1 (12 IN BY 18 IN) SHEET STIFF BLACK FELT
- 4 (12 IN) WOODEN DOWELS, ¼-INCH DIAMETER
- 2 (9 IN BY 12 IN) SHEETS PEEL-AND-STICK WHITE FELT

TOOLS:

- SCISSORS
- PENCIL
- RULER
- HOT GLUE GUN
- ULTRA FINE POINT BLACK PERMANENT MARKER

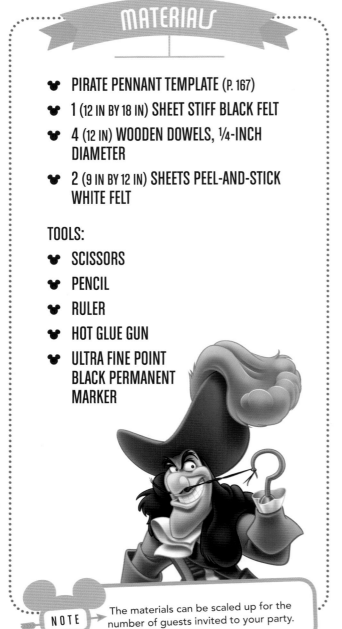

NOTE → The materials can be scaled up for the number of guests invited to your party.

After Captain Hook has successfully captured the Lost Boys and the Darlings, his crew performs a rousing number—complete with pirate flag pennants—extolling the benefits of the buccaneer lifestyle. Replicas of these pennants are ideal favors for a Captain Hook party, and they can be fashioned with wooden dowels, felt, and a steady hand. No cutlass or sailing skills required!

INSTRUCTIONS

STEP 1   Using the Pirate Pennant template on page 167, make a photocopy enlarging it 200 percent. Carefully cut out all of the shapes—this will be your master templates.

STEP 2   For each pennant, measure and cut a 6-by-9-inch rectangle of stiff black felt. Apply three parallel lines of hot glue along one narrow end of the black felt rectangle. The lines of glue should be close to the edge of the black felt rectangle and should be about ⅛ inch apart. Position a wooden dowel so that the top 6 inches of the dowel sit on top of the second line of hot glue. Carefully wrap the end of the black felt rectangle around the wooden dowel, rolling it in toward the center of the rectangle until the edge of the felt meets itself, making a complete casing around the wooden dowel. Set aside to dry.

STEP 3 While the hot glue is drying, trace the skull and two bones onto the sheet of white peel-and-stick felt. (It's best to trace on the felt's backing, so no stray pencil marks are left on the felt itself.) Cut out the shapes, and then use a ultra fine point black permanent marker to color in the eyes, nose, and mouth of the skull.

STEP 4 Once the hot glue is set, peel the backing off the skull and bone pieces and adhere them to the black rectangle, positioning the skull in the center, about ¼ inch from the top, and crossing the bones about ½ inch below the skull's chin. Yo ho, yo ho, your pirate pennant is finished!

TRICORN HAT BEAN AND CHEESE POCKETS

MAKES 8 POCKETS

MATERIALS

- 14 OZ FAVORITE RECIPE PIE CRUST OR PASTRY DOUGH, CHILLED (ENOUGH FOR A DOUBLE-CRUST 9 IN PIE)
- FLOUR, FOR ROLLING
- ½ C REFRIED BEANS
- ½ C SHREDDED MEXICAN-BLEND CHEESE
- 2 TBSP MILD SALSA
- SALT

TOOLS:

- BAKING SHEET
- PARCHMENT PAPER
- ROLLING PIN
- 1 (4 IN) ROUND CUTTER, OR BOWL OR CONTAINER OF SIMILAR SIZE
- 1 (3 IN) ROUND CUTTER, OR GLASS OF SIMILAR SIZE
- KNIFE

A traditional component of a pirate's ensemble, the tricorn hat was traditionally made out of either leather or felt. These edible tricorns are made from pastry dough and contain a savory bean-and-cheese filling that will satisfy little sailors. Captain Hook and his crew surely would have traded their hardtack biscuits for these tasty pockets any day!

INSTRUCTIONS

STEP 1 Preheat the oven to 400°F. Line a baking sheet with parchment paper. Divide the dough into two portions, one slightly larger than the other. On a lightly floured surface, roll out the slightly larger portion of dough to ⅛ in thickness. If the dough becomes sticky, sprinkle with flour and continue rolling. Using the 4-inch round cutter, cut out eight circles of dough. Transfer to parchment-lined baking sheet.

STEP 2 Roll out the slightly smaller portion of dough to a ⅛ in thickness, sprinkling with flour if it gets sticky. Using the 3-inch round cutter, cut out eight circles of dough. Set aside.

STEP 3 In a medium bowl, combine refried beans, cheese, and salsa. Stir to combine and add salt to taste. Place a tablespoon of the filling in the center of each 4-inch dough circle. Lay one of the 3-inch dough circles on top and press the edges down gently to seal all the way around the 3-inch circle. Use the side of a knife to slide underneath one side of the pastry, and fold one third of the edge up toward the center. Repeat with the other two sides, creating an equilateral triangle with a dome in the middle.

STEP 4 Place baking sheet in preheated oven and bake for 20 minutes, or until edges of pastries are golden brown. Cool for a few minutes before serving.

SKULL ROCK WATERMELON FRUIT SALAD

MATERIALS

- 1 SMALL, OVAL-SHAPED SEEDLESS WATERMELON
- 2 C FRESH PINEAPPLE CHUNKS
- 2 C HULLED AND HALVED STRAWBERRIES
- 2 C GREEN GRAPES
- OTHER FRUIT (OPTIONAL)

TOOLS:

- SHARP CARVING KNIFE
- MELON BALLER
- MARKER

MAKES 8 SERVINGS

A ghoulish island north of Mermaid Lagoon, Skull Rock is where Captain Hook carries out one of his vengeful schemes: he kidnaps Princess Tiger Lily and commands Mr. Smee to row them out to the rock, where he ties Tiger Lily to an anchor and questions her regarding Peter's whereabouts. Serving the dual purposes of centerpiece and nutritious snack, this fruit salad is served in a watermelon carved to look just like Never Land's most skeletal island!

INSTRUCTIONS

STEP 1 If the watermelon does not stand securely on one of its narrow ends, use a sharp carving knife to take a thin slice off the bottom, making it level.

STEP 2 Cut a slightly thicker slice off the opposite end. A circle of red watermelon flesh measuring 4 to 5 inches in diameter should now be visible. This will be the top of the skull. Use a melon baller to scoop out the red flesh of the watermelon into a large bowl. Be careful not to scoop too close to the white rind, as it provides stability for the structure, and take care not to scoop too close to the bottom, especially if a slice was taken off to level it.

STEP 3 Once the watermelon is hollow, use a marker to sketch out the face that you will carve out. Draw two large, rounded-square eyes; an upside-down heart in the center for a nose; and an open mouth revealing the upper row of teeth. Use a sharp carving knife to carefully cut out the shapes you have drawn, making sure to cut all the way through the skin and rind of the watermelon. Discard the cutouts.

STEP 4 Measure out 2 cups of the watermelon balls that were scooped out of the cavity and place in a separate large bowl. Add the pineapple chunks, halved strawberries, green grapes, and any other fruits that you'd like. Toss to combine.

STEP 5 Spoon the fruit salad into the cavity of the watermelon. Fill all the way to the top and reserve any leftover fruit salad to refill the cavity later on. Refrigerate both the carved watermelon and the remaining fruit salad until ready to serve.

PIRATE SHIP CAKE

A 13 X 9-INCH SHEET CAKE, TOPPED WITH A 7-INCH POUND CAKE SHIP

MATERIALS

- 1 (8½ IN BY 11 IN) SHEET WHITE PAPER
- 2 (12 IN) WOOD OR BAMBOO SKEWERS

INGREDIENTS:

- FAVORITE RECIPE FOR A 13 IN BY 9 IN SHEET CAKE (ANY FLAVOR)
- 1 (12 OZ) CONTAINER WHITE FROSTING
- BLUE FOOD COLORING (GEL OR DROPS)
- 1 (11 OZ) PREMADE POUND CAKE
- 1 (12 OZ) CONTAINER CHOCOLATE FROSTING
- 1 (4¼ OZ) TUBE YELLOW FROSTING

TOOLS:

- 13 IN BY 9 IN BAKING PAN
- OFFSET SPATULA OR CURVED KNIFE
- CUTTING BOARD
- SERRATED KNIFE
- STAR TIP FOR FROSTING TUBE
- WRITING TIP FOR FROSTING TUBE
- PENCIL
- RULER
- SCISSORS

Captain Hook's ship, the *Jolly Roger*, has everything needed for privateering purposes: a seaworthy hull, a sturdy set of sails, cannons, and a skull-adorned flag. However, the brig does not often encounter high-seas adventure, as the captain keeps it anchored in Never Land's Cannibal Cove while he plans his revenge on Peter Pan. Well, get ready for a high-*treat* adventure in your kitchen, because this pirate ship cake is about to set sail!

INSTRUCTIONS

STEP 1 Prepare and bake your favorite recipe for a 13-by-9-inch sheet cake. Cool for 15 minutes in the pan, then turn out onto a platter or tray and cool completely.

STEP 2 Place white frosting in a small mixing bowl. Add several drops of blue food coloring and stir until the frosting has a marbled appearance. Do not combine completely; you want your waves to look frothy and dynamic.

STEP 3 Using an offset spatula or curved knife, frost the top and sides of the cooled sheet cake with the blue icing. Use a swirling motion to create waves with dimension—do not smooth out the icing and make it flat.

STEP 4 To create the pirate ship, set the pound cake on a cutting board. Use a serrated knife to cut a thin sliver off the top to make it level. Determine which end will be the stern (back end) of the ship. Make a cut 2½ inches from the stern of the ship, completely spanning the width of the pound cake, cutting down about ¾ inch into the cake. Make another cut 2½ inches farther toward the bow (front end) of the ship, completely spanning the width of the pound cake, cutting down about ¾ inch into the cake. Insert the knife into the side of the cake, cutting parallel to the cutting board, to connect the first two cuts and remove a chunk of the cake. Save this piece of cake for later.

STEP 5 Shape the bow of the ship by cutting off the two corners at the front end. Cut vertically, at a 45-degree angle, from the center of the narrow dimension, creating a point for the bow.

STEP 6 Use the piece of cake reserved at the end of step 4 to create an elevated rear deck for the ship. The reserved piece should be about 3½ inches long and 2½ inches wide. Cut 1 inch off the width, making it 3½ inches long and 1½ inches wide. Use a knife to apply about a tablespoon of chocolate frosting atop the stern (back end) of the ship, spreading it evenly from side to side. Place the cut piece on top of the frosting so the long dimension of the piece is flush with the back end of the ship's body.

STEP 7 Once the ship is carved, set it on top of the iced sheet cake, centered in both dimensions. Frost the ship, covering all visible surfaces, with chocolate icing. Use the yellow icing to add decoration and embellishments such as a shell border (a star tip works well for this) and cannon ports (writing tip).

STEP 8 To create the mast and sails, measure and cut two 4-by-4½-inch rectangles and two 3½-by-4-inch rectangles from a sheet of white paper. Using the tip of the pencil, poke two holes in each rectangle—one on each end—centered in each long dimension, about ¼ inch from the edge.

STEP 9 Poke the pointed tip of a 12-inch skewer through one of the holes in one of the smaller sails. Slide the paper down the skewer a couple of inches and then thread the sail's second hole onto the skewer. Slide the smaller sail down the skewer so it stops about 1 inch from the end. Poke the tip through one of the holes in one of the larger sails. Slide the paper down the skewer a couple inches and then thread the

sail's second hole onto the skewer. Slide the larger sail down the skewer so it stops about 1 inch from the smaller sail. Repeat with the second skewer and second set of sails.

STEP 10 Insert the pointed tip of the first mast into the ship, centered, about 1½ inches back from the bow. Push it into the cake 1 to 2 inches. Insert the pointed tip of the second mast into the ship, centered, about 2½ inches behind the first mast. Push it into the cake 1 to 2 inches.

STEP 11 Keep the cake in a cool, dry place until ready to serve. The sheet cake and the ship itself can both be eaten; just be sure to remove the masts before cutting into the ship.

TEMPLATES

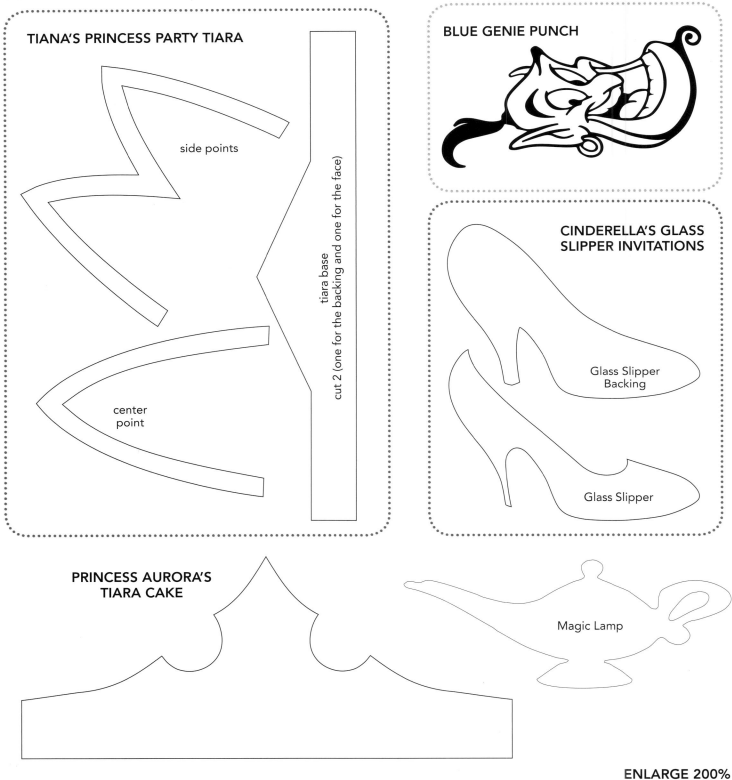

TIANA'S PRINCESS PARTY TIARA

side points

center point

tiara base
cut 2 (one for the backing and one for the face)

BLUE GENIE PUNCH

CINDERELLA'S GLASS SLIPPER INVITATIONS

Glass Slipper Backing

Glass Slipper

PRINCESS AURORA'S TIARA CAKE

Magic Lamp

ENLARGE 200%

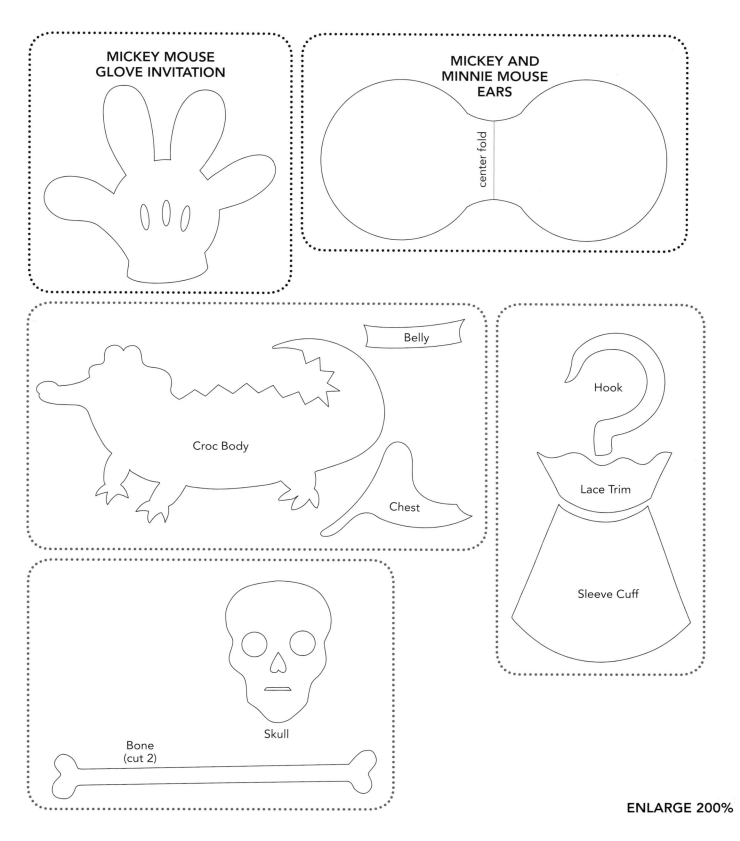

MICKEY MOUSE GLOVE INVITATION

MICKEY AND MINNIE MOUSE EARS

center fold

Belly

Croc Body

Chest

Hook

Lace Trim

Sleeve Cuff

Skull

Bone (cut 2)

ENLARGE 200%

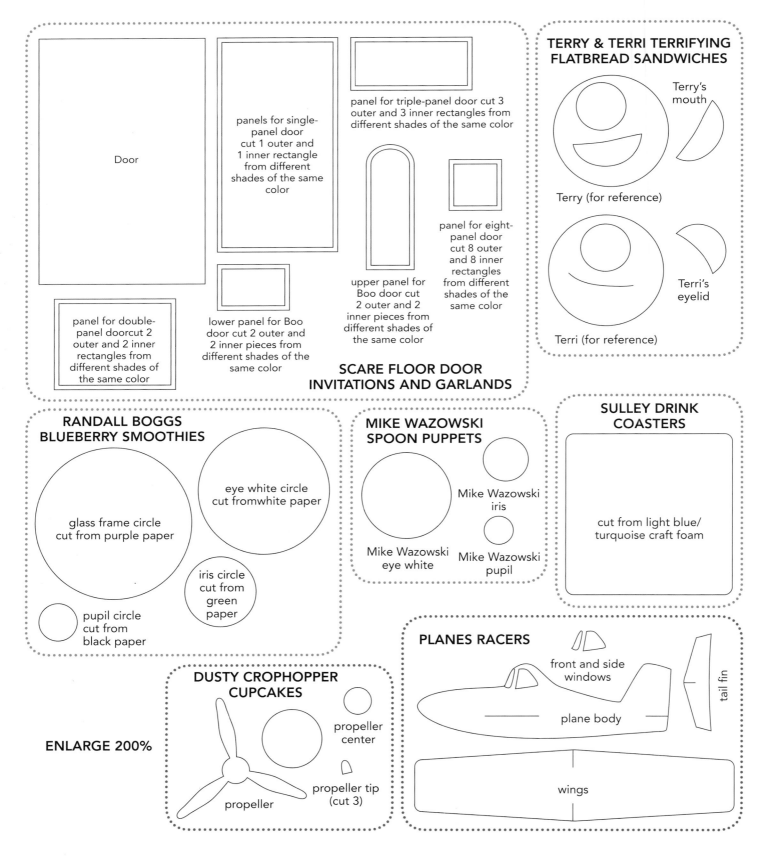

Door

panels for single-panel door cut 1 outer and 1 inner rectangle from different shades of the same color

panel for triple-panel door cut 3 outer and 3 inner rectangles from different shades of the same color

panel for eight-panel door cut 8 outer and 8 inner rectangles from different shades of the same color

upper panel for Boo door cut 2 outer and 2 inner pieces from different shades of the same color

lower panel for Boo door cut 2 outer and 2 inner pieces from different shades of the same color

panel for double-panel doorcut 2 outer and 2 inner rectangles from different shades of the same color

SCARE FLOOR DOOR INVITATIONS AND GARLANDS

TERRY & TERRI TERRIFYING FLATBREAD SANDWICHES

Terry's mouth

Terry (for reference)

Terri's eyelid

Terri (for reference)

RANDALL BOGGS BLUEBERRY SMOOTHIES

glass frame circle cut from purple paper

eye white circle cut fromwhite paper

iris circle cut from green paper

pupil circle cut from black paper

MIKE WAZOWSKI SPOON PUPPETS

Mike Wazowski iris

Mike Wazowski eye white

Mike Wazowski pupil

SULLEY DRINK COASTERS

cut from light blue/ turquoise craft foam

PLANES RACERS

front and side windows

tail fin

plane body

wings

DUSTY CROPHOPPER CUPCAKES

propeller center

propeller tip (cut 3)

propeller

ENLARGE 200%

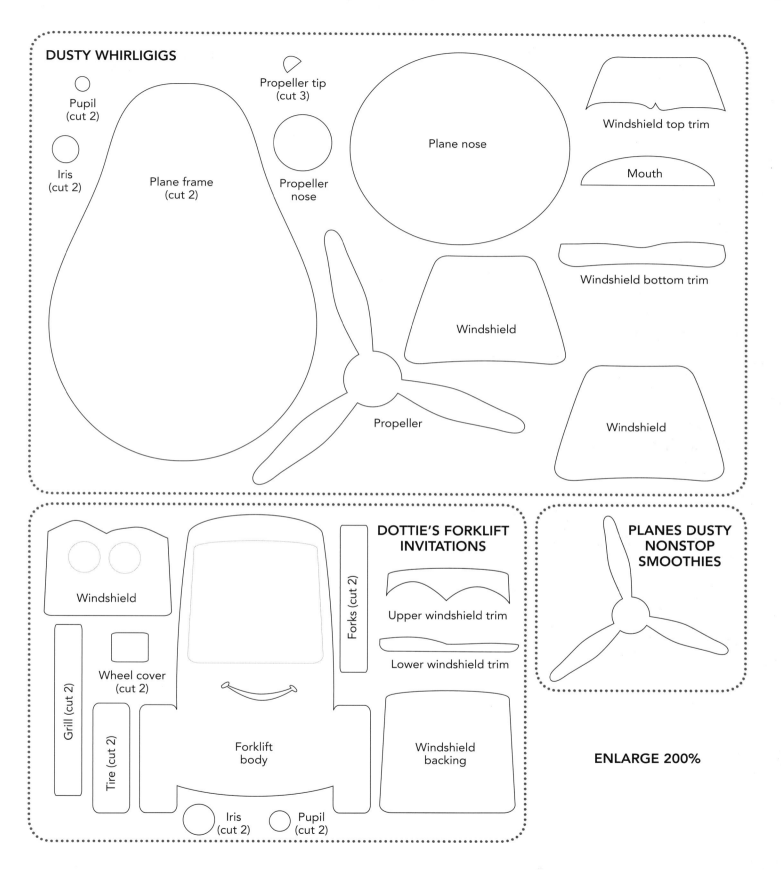

DUSTY WHIRLIGIGS

Pupil
(cut 2)

Iris
(cut 2)

Plane frame
(cut 2)

Propeller tip
(cut 3)

Propeller
nose

Plane nose

Propeller

Windshield

Windshield

Windshield top trim

Mouth

Windshield bottom trim

**DOTTIE'S FORKLIFT
INVITATIONS**

Windshield

Wheel cover
(cut 2)

Grill (cut 2)

Tire (cut 2)

Forklift
body

Forks (cut 2)

Upper windshield trim

Lower windshield trim

Windshield
backing

Iris
(cut 2)

Pupil
(cut 2)

**PLANES DUSTY
NONSTOP
SMOOTHIES**

ENLARGE 200%

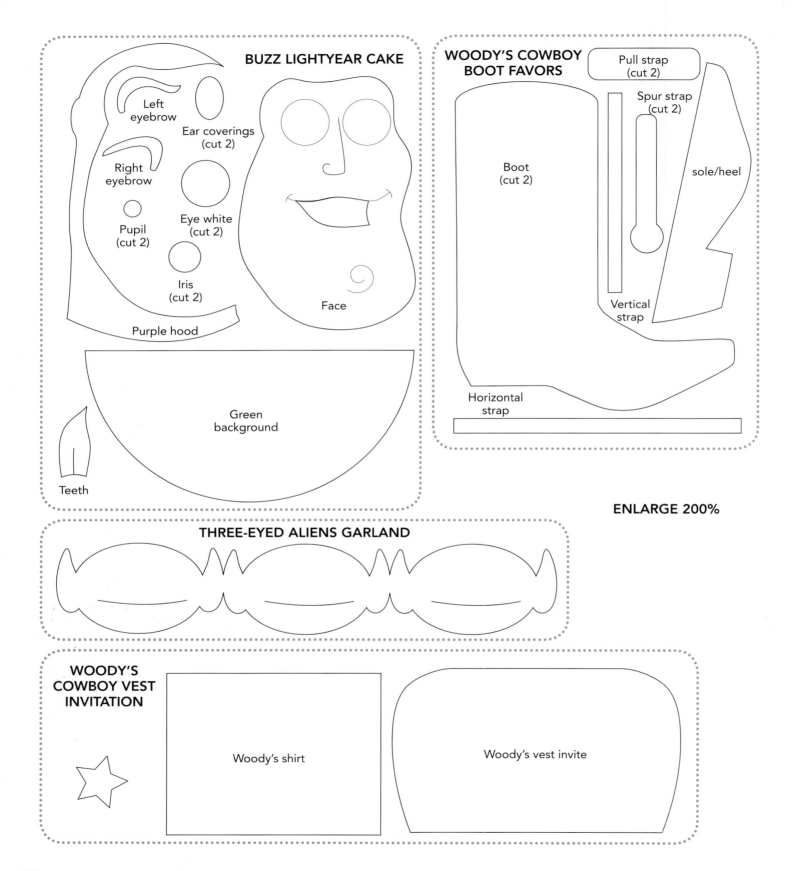

BUZZ LIGHTYEAR CAKE

Left eyebrow

Ear coverings (cut 2)

Right eyebrow

Pupil (cut 2)

Eye white (cut 2)

Iris (cut 2)

Face

Purple hood

Green background

Teeth

WOODY'S COWBOY BOOT FAVORS

Pull strap (cut 2)

Spur strap (cut 2)

Boot (cut 2)

sole/heel

Vertical strap

Horizontal strap

ENLARGE 200%

THREE-EYED ALIENS GARLAND

WOODY'S COWBOY VEST INVITATION

Woody's shirt

Woody's vest invite

PIN THE HAMMER ON
FIX-IT FELIX, JR.

"I'M GONNA WRECK IT!"
PENTHOUSE PIÑATA

ENLARGE 200%

INDEX